Your Towns and Cities in the

Bath

in the Great War

Your Towns and Cities in the Great War

Bath
in the Great War

Derek Tait

Pen & Sword
MILITARY

First published in Great Britain in 2015 by
PEN & SWORD MILITARY
an imprint of
Pen and Sword Books Ltd
47 Church Street
Barnsley
South Yorkshire S70 2AS

ISBN 978 1 47382 349 5

Printed and bound in England
by CPI Group (UK) Ltd, Croydon, CR0 4YY

Pen & Sword Books Ltd incorporates the imprints of
Pen & Sword Archaeology, Atlas, Aviation, Battleground, Discovery,
Family History, History, Maritime, Military, Naval, Politics, Railways,
Select, Social History, Transport, True Crime, and Claymore Press,
Frontline Books, Leo Cooper, Praetorian Press, Remember When,
Seaforth Publishing and Wharncliffe.

For a complete list of Pen and Sword titles please contact
Pen and Sword Books Limited
47 Church Street, Barnsley, South Yorkshire, S70 2AS, England
E-mail: enquiries@pen-and-sword.co.uk
Website: www.pen-and-sword.co.uk

Contents

Acknowledgements

Thanks to 'thardy' (Flickr), Daisy Parker, Derek Parker, Benjamin Pile, Alan Tait, Ellen Tait, Tina Cole and Tilly Barker.

Thanks also to the helpful and friendly team at Pen and Sword, including Roni Wilkinson, Matt Jones, Jon Wilkinson, Diane Wordsworth, Katie Eaton, Laura Lawton, Jodie Butterwood, Tara Moran and Lisa Goose.

CHAPTER ONE

1914 – Eager for a Fight

Rising tensions in Europe and the assassination of Franz Ferdinand in Sarajevo led to Austria-Hungary's declaration of war on Serbia. This in turn led to the Central Powers, which included Germany and Austria-Hungary, and the Allies, which included the British Empire, the French Republic and the Russian Empire, to declare war on each other, which led to the commencement of the First World War on 28 July 1914.

On 4 August, newspapers posted announcements in their windows stating that Britain had declared war on Germany.

People of foreign descent were quickly rounded up and

Archduke Franz Ferdinand of Austria. Ferdinand's assassination in Sarajevo on 28 June 1914 lead to Austria-Hungary's declaration of war on Serbia, which ultimately led to the beginning of the First World War.

A horse being loaded on board ship. Hundreds of thousands of horses were requisitioned during the war and many died in combat. Some, however, did survive and were brought back to Britain, and a few were cared for by animal charities.

detained. Anyone with a German sounding accent soon came under suspicion of being a spy.

The railways were taken under government control under the Regulations of Forces Act of 1871. Local businesses were asked to supply motor vehicles for use by the army and businesses in and around Bath were asked to supply horses.

Horses fared badly at the Front. Many were killed by artillery fire and were affected by skin conditions and poison gas. Hundreds of

Two soldiers take care of one of their horses. Casualties amongst horses in the artillery and transport divisions were high but soldiers of the Army Veterinary Corps worked hard to relieve any suffering. All wounds and injuries were carefully treated. Here, a sergeant sews up a wound on a horse's nose.

thousands of horses died during the conflict. Many horses were requisitioned from British civilians. However, Lord Kitchener stated that no horse under 15 hands should be confiscated. This was because many children showed concern about the welfare of their ponies.

Nine employees at the Bath Electricity Works who were in the Army Reserves were called up on Wednesday 5 August and many more waited ready to be called. The chairman of the committee (Alderman H. T. Hatt) addressed the nine reservists. He told them that they should leave feeling assured that he would do everything in his power to keep their jobs open until they returned. He also stated that he would do all he could to see that their wives and children were well looked after and was certain he would have the full support of the city council.

Many of the staff at the Bath Post Office responded to the king's proclamation calling-up reserves. The work of the post office was expected to be disorganised at first by the loss of men but

Lord Kitchener. Field Marshal Horatio Herbert Kitchener, 1st Earl Kitchener, played a vital role in the early part of the First World War. However, he died on 5 June 1916 long before the end of the conflict.

Many men rush to enlist, 1914. As war was announced, men of all ages were keen to enlist and showed much patriotism. Many saw it as an adventure, a way to escape unemployment or their humdrum daily lives. Most thought that the war wouldn't last long and would be over by Christmas.

temporary postmen were employed generally from those who usually took on the work at Christmas time.

Also on Wednesday 5 August, at the central police station, Chief Inspector Barter bade farewell to fourteen members of the city police force, who left with the reservists. At 9 am, the men left with their kit and attended parade in the parade room.

The *Bath Chronicle* reported:

> *Having been photographed and formed into line, Chief Inspector Barter told the men that this would be the last opportunity they would have of answering the roll call in Bath probably for some time to come. They had all been called to answer the King's proclamation and he was glad to say that they had all responded as one man. He wished them God-speed, good luck and a speedy return. He was sure that they would uphold the dignity of the Bath Police Force. Three cheers were given for the Reservists and the National Anthem was sung.*

The mayor (Dr Preston King) gave a personal send-off to the police reservists on Wednesday afternoon at the train station. The platform was crowded shortly before their departure at 2.30 pm. Among the members of the corporation present were the mayor, Alderman Hatt, Major-General Bradshaw, Mr P. Jackman, Mr T. T. Stone and Commander Bishop. A large number of the police force, both in and out of uniform also turned out to cheer them on.

Chief Inspector Barter introduced the mayor to the men, who shook hands with each of them. The mayor said he had come down to wish them God speed and said they were fighting in a war that had been thrust upon them. He said that Englishmen loved peace but they loved honour more. He continued that he was confident the honour of the country would be safe in their hands and the great traditions of the British Army would be worthily upheld by them. This was met by cheers from the crowd. After several more speeches, the men departed amid cheers from onlookers and fellow policemen who held up their helmets as a final salute to their comrades. The newspaper reported that a number of female relatives and friends were on the platform and there was some sadness.

The 1st Field Company of the Wessex Royal Engineers returned to

Bath from Bulford Camp on Wednesday 5 August before departing that evening. The men were said to have had a long journey getting to Bath and were described as looking dog tired, with some who had not slept for two or three nights. They had waited for their train to Bath from Tuesday morning and were out in the wettest weather. When they arrived in Bath, their great coats were soaked through and some said that the water had been ankle deep.

The *Bath Chronicle* reported:

ROUSED!

A patriotic postcard showing a lion and Union Jack with the caption 'Roused!'

At Bath Station, the band was drawn up at the foot of the goods slope, whilst the wagons loaded up the baggage for the depot. Major Dutton was present. A large crowd took interest in watching the men march down and the limbers and wagons brought into Dorchester Street. The men snatched a few brief hours of home comforts before they re-assembled at the depot to march to the station.

The men, 113 in number, paraded at the Drill Hall, Upper Bristol Road, shortly before six. The officers who accompanied the men were Major Dutton, Captain Harvey and Lieutenant Pitt. Lieutenant Harbutt, with an advance party, left earlier in the day to take over stores. The streets through which the men passed on their way to the station were lined by interested spectators and the approach of the contingent to the GWR station was signalled by loud cheering. The entraining of the men was witnessed by hundreds of people. At 6.40, the train steamed out of the station amid cheers and the waving of hats and handkerchiefs.

The mounted men leave on Saturday with wagons and stores and the headquarters will then be made a depot for enlisting recruits.

The men who were mobilised on Wednesday received their bounty of £5 a man.

In August, the 4th Somersets were ordered on garrison service after training on Salisbury Plain. After travelling for twenty-three hours, they reached their destination in the heavy rain. Because of this, they were temporarily housed at the nearby barracks before going to camp. All men were said to be in excellent health.

During August, it was reported that there had been a spy scare in Bath. On Thursday 6 August, a rumour circulated that a German spy disguised as a woman had been arrested in Westgate Street. Later, it was learned that the spy was actually a young Welshman who, for reasons known only to himself, had decided to dress as a woman wearing a straw hat and veil together with a long dressing gown of white and red material. He was detained by the police but refused to give his name and address. He later admitted that he had disguised himself for a joke and a wager. He was eventually released.

MAYOR OF BATH'S APPEAL

TO YOUNG MEN TO JOIN THE TERRITORIALS.

To the Editor " Bath Weekly Chronicle."

Sir,—I wish, through the medium of your paper, to make a most earnest appeal to all those of our young men who have not already done so to at once join the Territorial Forces. There can be no two questions as to the serious nature of the crisis which we are approaching. Our very existence as a nation will shortly be put to the test. Our Colonies are showing the spirit of true patriotism by the course that they are taking in promising aid, and I am sure that those in the Old Country will not hesitate to maintain and hold what their fathers died to gain.

It is in no spirit of panic that I write, and make this appeal. If we wait till the actual need of trained men is upon us, there will then, it is true, be a risk of panic. Let us remember that we are Englishmen, and keep calm in the time of danger; but above all let us do our duty.

PRESTON KING, Mayor.

The mayor of Bath's appeal to young men, 1914. Preston King requested that all fit and eligible men join the Territorial Forces. He stated 'Let us remember that we are Englishmen and keep calm in the time of danger but above all, let us do our duty'.

The *Bath Chronicle and Weekly Gazette* of Saturday 8 August 1914 reported:

> *Great Britain has declared war against Germany and has joined France, Russia and Belgium in their resistance to the infamous designs of the 'mad dog of Europe'. Serbia is also at war with Austria, Germany's ally. Thus all Europe is ablaze. Already there has been severe fighting. The Belgians, with magnificent heroism, have repulsed the German invaders with heavy loss, in one battle alone the Germans leaving 8,000 dead. Unhappily, Britain has met with a naval disaster, HMS Amphion having been blown up on Thursday by a mine with a loss of 121 lives. One of the officers among the dead, Staff-Paymaster Gedge, was a nephew of Dr Preston King, the Mayor of Bath.*
>
> *The war has caused phenomenal activity in many phases of local life. During the week, Bath Territorials and Reservists have been called up and many of them dispatched, amid enthusiastic scenes, to various destinations. Not only that, but great additional activity has been occasioned at the passage through the city of enormous fleets of heavy motor vehicles which have been commandeered from London traders and others and sent to Bristol Docks to assist in the transport of food and materials for the troops.*
>
> *Large numbers of horses have been seized for military purposes in Bath and the surrounding districts. In the earlier part of the week, food prices rose rapidly but the Government yesterday fixed maximum prices for food-stuffs and matters are beginning to take a normal course. Special editions of the Bath Chronicle are being published each evening giving the latest war news and each evening the city streets have presented animated scenes, large crowds waiting till after midnight to learn the latest tidings. Locally, there has been a loyal response to the King's call for 100,000 more Territorials and recruiting is actively proceeding.*

One of the crew on the ill-fated *Amphion* was William Ernest Hicks of 9 Mount Pleasant, Snow Hill, Walcot. Hicks was a signal boy who had been in the service for two years. His parents were anxious as they had heard no news of his whereabouts from the Admiralty. A friend of

Kitchener's call to arms. The great numbers of men needed for the army were brought together by regular appeals by the authorities for young men to join-up. The campaign went on around the country. This photo shows a recruitment speaker surrounded by flags and posters. On the chairs are the various uniforms of the army and the speaker is compelling young men to put one on rather than wearing civilian attire.

Hicks, also from Bath, named Comley was also on board the *Amphion* and was also missing.

Twenty men working at James Colmer Limited intimated their willingness to serve in the army. The directors of the firm stated that if the men were called upon to serve that their jobs would be kept open for them.

Meanwhile at Bath Guildhall, two royal proclamations were posted. One forbade trading with Germany and the other said that no contraband was to be carried by British ships.

A letter appeared in the *Bath Weekly Chronicle* under the headline 'A Message to Young Men.' It read:

> *Sir,- I cannot help commenting upon this following in your issue of last night.*
>
> *The young men in the crowd formed up in processions, and headed by waving flags, they marched up and down Westgate Street singing 'God Save the King,' 'England expects that every man', 'The Anchor's Weighed' and other songs.*
>
> *How typical of the age. Had these young men accepted a duty imposed upon them by their manhood, how much more to their credit if they were now capable of bearing arms in defence of their homes and their kin than to be shouting, as they apparently were, in a time of sorrow and anxiety to so many.*
>
> *Captain L K Bunting.*

Towards the end of August, the mayoress took charge of the voluntary work being done by women of the city to provide underclothing for soldiers in the field and in hospital. Most of the items being made by the Needlework Guild were delivered to the Red Cross Society. Efforts

were concentrated by the organisation to equip a base hospital of 200 beds within the city or elsewhere. This was a large undertaking and meant the supplying of bedlinen, pillows, nightshirts, towels, bed jackets, nightingales and operating overalls for surgeons and nurses as well as a vast quantity of bandages. The ground floor of 55

Women look for news of their men. Wives and mothers eagerly scanned any notices posted containing lists of casualties. A crowd would gather when any new news was issued. Daily columns of deceased and wounded servicemen also appeared in local newspapers.

Pulteney Street was taken over by the Red Cross Society for the purpose.

The Bath Motor Cyclists War Service Corps, whose headquarters were at the Castle Hotel, mobilised on Thursday 3 September at the Sawclose. The response was a parade of over thirty motorcycles. A large number of people witnessed the proceedings. The organisation had come into existence as a direct consequence of the war. By working with the local police, the motorcyclists were able to carry out important patrol work, day and night, on the outskirts of Bath. A letter from a Captain Bunting requested that one of the cyclists be attached to the Somerset Light Infantry Depot as an orderly. One of the duties of the motorcyclists was to patrol the reservoirs at Monkswood, Oakford, Batheaston and Charlcombe to check that all was well with the guards there and to deliver and receive messages.

At the meeting, a number of new members joined the association and signed forms for both foreign and home service.

An article appeared in the local newspaper of 5 September regarding football and the war. Under the heading 'Bath Club's Patriotic Decision', it read:

> *A fully attended meeting of the Bath Football Club Committee was held at the Red House Restaurant on Tuesday evening to consider the position created by the war.*

Rifle or Football——Which ?

> *The Chairman (Mr Arthur Taylor) read a letter inviting the Club's representatives to the conference he has convened at the Guildhall on Friday evening, and expressing his own strong opinion that when the nation's existence was at stake, games in which active young men are engaged should be suspended, as they were needed for military service. Other letters of a similar nature were read by the Chairman who expressed entire concurrence with the views of the writers.*
>
> *Mr G A Roberts, the honorary*

A notice in the Devon and Exeter Gazette of Saturday 5 September 1914 carried the headline 'Rifle or football'. The newspaper said it would be disgraceful if football continued during the war and Lord Roberts called for it to be stopped.

secretary, then moved the following resolution:- 'That having regard to the grave crisis through which our country is passing, and the urgent call to every eligible man to take up arms for Britain's honour and security, this committee decides that no matches be played before Christmas and that in December the situation be further considered. The committee feel sure that the many members of the club will appreciate the patriotic motive inspiring this resolution and rally to their support when under happier auspices, it may be possible to resume club games.'

This was seconded by the Chairman and carried unanimously without discussion.

A postcard featuring women munition workers. Female workers played a vital role at home during the conflict.

On Monday 14 September, a Mrs Allen of 34 Thomas Street, Walcot, celebrated her 100th birthday. She was born in the year before the Battle of Waterloo. It was said she enjoyed good health although her sight and hearing were slightly fading. Newspaper reports said she took a great interest in the war.

On 19 September, Major J. M. T. Reilly in charge of the recruiting office, announced that during the five weeks since the mobilisation of the British forces, 900 men had been enlisted in Bath and had been accepted for the regular army. He stated that the demand for men had by no means ceased and he hoped to get the total enlisted up to 1,000. In addition to the 900, a large number of Bathonians had also enrolled in the Territorials – 4th Somersets, North Somerset Yeomanry, Wessex Royal Engineers and RAMC. Almost 1,000 men had enlisted from the city in these various regiments.

An active service battalion of the 4th Somersets had been formed with a total strength of 1,500 men.

Major Reilly stated that recruitment for the Somerset Light Infantry had now been completed with two new battalions, each of 1,000 men, having been raised for Lord Kitchener's Army as well as a Special Reserve Battalion, containing 1,000 men, for the Somerset Territorials.

Forthcoming attractions to the city for the second half of September included 'Carlton', at the Palace. He was billed as the 'Premier Comic Conjurer'. His speciality involved hypnotism, which was described as 'his laughing success of the century'.

On Thursday 22 October, a whist drive was held at Shapland's Cafe in Stall Street, in connection with the Bath and District Devonians Society. There were thirty-four tables and the event saw Mr T. Wills,

A busy scene showing Milsom Street in Bath. On the left can be seen the Midland Bank.

Milsom Street, Bath.

A busy scene, featuring mainly women and children, of Union Street in Bath. On the right of the photo can be seen J. Hepworth and Son Ltd, manufacturers of home and colonial clothing.

the president of the association, act as MC. The profits were to be used to provide tobacco and comforts for the Devonshire Regiment at the Front. It was hoped that the total would come to £10. A ladies' working party was formed in connection with the society and another was to be held on 19 November with the proceeds going to the Mayor of Bath's Fund.

On the evening of Tuesday 3 November, a concert was held at the Livingstone Hotel, Oldfield Park, in aid of the local war relief fund. Before the concert, the Oldfield Park Military Band played a selection of music outside the hotel. A collection raised ten shillings and ten pence. The concert was chaired by Councillor W. Dawe, who gave a stirring patriotic address. Mr W. E. Angell played the piano and songs were delivered by various local singers. A large number of people attended and the concert was much enjoyed. The proceeds of the concert amounted to £2 13s 19d, which was made up of the sale of programmes, £1 6s 6d; collected by Oldfield Park Band, 10s 10d; sale of a marrow (which was presented by a member), 2s; and a collection in the room, 14s 5d.

During November, Mr J. Harris of Monkton Combe received a postcard from his son, Private P. Harris, saying that he was quite well but was now a prisoner-of-war in Germany. Private Harris had been reported missing on 25 August.

On Thursday 12 November, Madame Clara Butt gave a patriotic concert in Bristol where a Miss Collier recited *The Day* by Henry Chappell.

PC Howells of the Bath City Police Force was reported invalided home during November. His colleagues, PC Skeates, Maule and Harding, were all said to be quite well.

Mr Selman of 7 Hopmead Buildings, Twerton, received a letter from his son, Fred, who was a sadler in the 5th Dragoon Guards. He lay wounded in the Duchess of Westminster's Hospital, which he described as 'a French casino and my ward is the gambling room'. His letter went on to say:

I am so sorry to say that the old 5th copped out very bad last week and we had been so lucky. I know one thing and that is for every one we lost, the Germans lost four, and I don't suppose we should have lost half as many only for a horrible mistake, but I can't tell you about that. I hope you don't belong to the 'All is Lost League.' Anyone you hear talking down-hearted, just give him a kick, and tell him to join Kitchener's Army.

On Saturday 14 November, the *Bath Chronicle* reported on the work done by Americans on behalf of the British. Under the headline 'Christmas Gifts for Orphan Children', the story read:

Mrs Van Sommer, of Meadville, Lansdowne, kindly forwards us a cutting from a leading American journal drawing attention to a movement by American women to send Christmas gifts to children orphaned through the war.

Somebody has calculated that by Christmas, 1,000,000 children will be fatherless because of the war.

It is to bring a little Christmas joy to these orphans that almost 2,000,000 American women have started a fund to send Yuletide remembrances abroad early in December. Contributions are being received by one newspaper in all the principal cities of the United States.

The Red Cross Society is interested in the work and will help with the distribution of gifts.

The Christmas packages are to go to all the nations at war, the offering being strictly impartial.

On 21 November, it was reported that two ladies, two monkeys and a French poodle, complete with a barrel organ, would be visiting Bath as part of a scheme to aid the Belgian Food Fund. The ladies, who were well-known in Worcestershire and Gloucestershire, had already successfully collected money in other parts of the country before coming to Bath. They had already sent £50 for the fund to the Belgian Minister in London.

An animated scene, complete with trams and carts, in High Street, Bath around the time of the First World War.

On 5th December, the *Bath Chronicle* reported on the Athletes' Volunteer Force. The formation of the force had met with great success and membership had grown rapidly with the result that there were 600 members who were divided into sixteen squads. Major Brewster offered to form a squad at Odd Down, if there was enough interest, and arrange drills in the schools twice a week.

Mr Charles Jones, the keeper of the Warleigh Ferry, suffered the bereavement of his son, Chief Petty Officer Charles Jones, who was on board the ill-fated HMS *Bulwark,* which was blown up in Sheerness Harbour.

The 'Local War Items' column in the newspaper for 5 December reported:

> *Lieutenant R W Shannon, who has been at home in Bath for some time, resting from the hardships of the war, expects to return to the Front in the course of a few days. The Lieutenant, who is now looking extremely fit and well again, informs us that he was in the trenches for four days but took part in only one bayonet charge, not several, as had been suggested in an account previously published. The party he was with was under continual bombardment and Lieutenant Shannon was almost buried in his trench from the effects of one of the German shells. Lieutenant Shannon received his commission last January.*

During December, Sergeant Bert Reakes of the Army Service Corps wrote home to his mother thanking her for sending him the Bath newspaper. In his letter, he wrote:

> *Bath is a very military sort of place just now, isn't it? I read nearly every line of the* Chronicle. *There must be a lot of Germans in the world for this war to keep on like it is. We are getting as callous as butchers. The most sickening sights don't make us take our pipes out of our mouths. Homes, nothing but heaps of smouldering ruins, are often passed without remark. I never thought that one could get really used to what we have. I often think though, 'What if this happened in England?' A trip round here by some of the thousands of men who are content to watch football matches would make them rush like maniacs to the recruiter, once they had seen what could happen to England. It's awful!*

In the week before Christmas, it was reported that Mr Charles Gibbs of Bath had paid a visit to his son, Sergeant C. Gibbs of the North Somerset Yeomanry, who was now in hospital in Brighton. He was said to be much improved since his admission but it would take him a long time to recover because he'd received a serious shell wound in the back.

The Bath Society of Devonians, through Mrs T. Wills, sent to the

The Bath Chronicle and Weekly Gazette of Saturday 12 December 1914 published a photo of Lance-Corporal A. Besant with the caption: 'Duke of Cornwall's LI. Killed on a date not yet ascertained. Deceased, who was unmarried, was a conductor on the Weston route of the Bath Electric Tramways Ltd. He was a native of Calne and lived at 4 Worcester Buildings, Larkhall, with a married brother also on military service.'

Private W. M. Follon of the 1st Devon Regiment (standing) who died from wounds received in action. His mother lived at 1 The Ambury, Bath. Seated is Private T. Goodman of the same regiment. Bath Chronicle and Weekly Gazette of Saturday 12 December 1914.

mayoress (Mrs Kirk Owen) a large number of knitted articles for the Devon regiments at the Front. The mayoress wrote a letter to Mrs Wills to thank her. It read:

The Bath Devonian Society's parcel has reached me and I must congratulate you on the splendid result of your efforts. The articles shall be sent to the front immediately.

A special Chocolate Day received contributions for the sailors and soldiers abroad and was packed at the Bristol headquarters of the Navy League. A large

Gunner Frederick James Clarke, of the RFA, who was killed at Ypres on 31 October 1914. Gunner Clarke was the son of Mr James Clarke of 2 Philip Street, Bath, who had another son serving with the 4th Somersets. Bath Chronicle and Weekly Gazette of Saturday 12 December 1914.

The death was announced of Private William Brewer of the Wiltshire Regiment in the Bath Chronicle and Weekly Gazette of Saturday 12 December 1914. Private Brewer was exceedingly well-known in local football circles. Formerly, he was captain of Chippenham Town. An old Territorial, he re-enlisted on the outbreak of war. Private Brewer was the cousin of Mr Manns, who was formerly the secretary of the Bath Thursday club. Private Brewer was killed in action.

consignment was forwarded to the Front, including twenty-four cases to the Somerset Light Infantry and twelve cases to the North Somerset Yeomanry.

On 19 December, the *Bath Chronicle* carried a short article under the headline 'Bath Boxer at the Front'. It read:

Driver A Jerry, of the Army Service Corps, writes home to his employer, Mr W T Winstone, of Brougham Hayes, Bath, in good spirits but evidently he has not received several letters sent to him by his wife and others in Bath. He says: 'I do not know if I will be home next month or not, or whether they will keep me out here. As

This photo appeared in the Bath Chronicle and Weekly Gazette of Saturday 12 December 1914 under the headline: 'Bath Resident's Four Sons with the Colours.' The caption read: 'Mr A. Godwin, of 1 Norfolk Crescent, Bath, an old resident of the city, has four sons serving in the Army. Two of them, Arthur, aged 28, and Jack, aged 26, have given up good appointments in Winnipeg and have come back to the old country with the Canadian Expeditionary Force. The eldest, Frank, is in the 1st Wessex RE and the youngest, Reg, is at Prior Park with the 1st Somerset Reserves.'

you know, I finish my reserve on 20th January. I hope they will send
me home so that I may be able to take my clothes off when I have a
sleep; it won't be half a change!'

At the end of December, the local newspapers reported that helpers of
the Bath Santa Claus scheme had visited the poorer areas of the city
collecting children's names and addresses. The scheme had continued
for nineteen years, but there was a worry that with the outbreak of war
it wouldn't continue. Part of the premises of Messrs Hooper and Dark
were used for the collection and sorting of goods, and for three days,
packers were engaged in making up suitable presents for each child.
The previous Christmas, 1,300 gifts had been distributed although, for
the first time in 1914, children from Belgium were also catered for.

The *Bath Chronicle* reported:

Shortly before two o'clock on Thursday, the Santa Claus procession
was ready to depart from Messrs. Hooper and Dark's. The gifts had
been loaded into four vans, which were under the superintendence
of members of their committee and helpers. The van which was
intended for the Dolemeads had the misfortune to meet with a
breakdown and, as a consequence, the children from that
neighbourhood were invited to come in person to Messrs. Hooper
and Dark's and to carry their gifts home. Alderman Benshaw had
charge of their district and saw that the parcels reached the proper
persons.

To relieve the curiosity of those who would like to know what the
parcels contained, it may be stated that each child's present was of
a three-fold character comprising an article of wear, a toy and
something to eat.

Christmas celebrations included entertainment for soldiers and refugees
in Bath. The *Bath Chronicle* noted:

The ladies who organized the treat for our Belgian friends in Bath
have every reason to feel satisfied with the complete success of their
effort – they gave unbounded pleasure to those for whom the
entertainment was arranged. All the Belgian refugees in and around
Bath participated in the enjoyment provided, as well as the wives of
British soldiers and sailors who attended the Women's Club at

Citizen House. At five o'clock, a bountiful tea was served at the Assembly Rooms where the programme opened. The guests numbered between 300 and 400. Much fun was afforded by the crackers and parlour fireworks. In the Ball Room, the chief attraction were seven resplendent Christmas trees, quite fifteen feet high, decorated in the most fascinating manner, a brilliant effect being produced by the numerous coloured electric glows introduced among the branches. At the base of the trees, which had been supplied by Mr. W. H. Coles of the Nurseries, Weston Road, were piled the gifts. But before their distribution began, there was a delightful preliminary. Christmas bells rang out from the minstrels' gallery and while the boys of the Abbey Choir sang a carol, St. Nicholas (or Santa Claus as we know him) paraded the room, attended by a train of merry gnomes, in correct costume, carrying antique lanterns. The patron saint of boys (impersonated by the Rev. H. L. Maynard) spoke in French to the company, his remarks (translated into English) being 'Good evening all, I have just arrived from Belgium after a terrible voyage. With great difficulty, I escaped from the trenches. You see this little hole in my coat – a bullet went through my sleeve, another struck my boot, so I am walking a little lame. A shell burst over my head, so I am a little bit deaf. Submarines and torpedoes tried to sink my ship and last, and worst of all, my donkey was drowned. But it is well worth undergoing hardship to come here and find you, my young friends. St. Nicholas salutes you; he is the saint of young people. England, the protector and friend of the unfortunate, pays homage to the children of heroes. May the future make you worthy of your noble parents and bring you back to your country, restored and more beautiful, more happy, more honoured than ever.' (Cheers.)

The 200 Belgian guests and the 130 Bath mothers and their children were allowed near the Christmas trees as many onlookers cheered loudly as Belgian soldiers, many crippled by the war, joked with one another whilst wearing coloured paper hats and tinsel chains. After the children had been laden with dolls and toys, the adults received gifts of clothes from a table surrounded by the Girl Guides. After tea, the guests adjourned to the Theatre Royal where a concert had been arranged by Miss Vera John. A ladies' orchestra, under Miss Lucy King, who presided at the piano, played a selection of popular music. Sergeant Harvey and Sergeant Farley, of the 10th Devons, gave their own rendition of *Tipperary*, which went:

It's a long march into Berlin,
  It's a long way to go;
  It's a long march into Berlin
  For John Bull and Co.
  When we get the Kaiser,
  Then we'll pull his hair;
  There'll be long, long faces on the Germans
  When the Devons get there.

The audience, including the Belgians, sang the familiar words to the song. The concert finished with a patriotic theme, with ladies representing the Allies swathed in their national flags who were grouped with Britannia, in costume, with a Jack Tar on the right and a Tommy on the left. Belgium, Russia, France, Japan and Serbia were also represented. Renditions of *Rule Britannia* and *God Save the King* concluded the evening.

On 26 December, under the headline 'Bath's Reason to be Proud', the news of a message received from a sergeant at the Front was published. The story read:

Colour-Sergeant Boundy, of the Recruiting Office, Bath, has received a postcard from Sergeant Neville, of the 1st Somersets, with a postmark from North France, in which the writer says:

'Still going strong. The regiment has distinguished itself out here and helped to put more than one spoke in the Kaiser's wheel. You

may tell Bathonians they have reason to be proud of their county regiment and the Westcountry of the units of the 4th Division which belong to them. Best wishes to yourself

Miss Irene Millard, who played the principal boy in Cinderella in the pantomime at the Theatre Royal in December 1914. The show was described as 'bright and enjoyable' and attracted very large audiences. The Canadian troops in Bath attended a special performance of the pantomime during January 1915.

and Mrs Boundy and the boys from the firing line. Yours sincerely,
Harry.

Sergeant Neville had been wounded once or twice, but not
seriously, and he will not leave the trenches.'

The pantomime for Christmas 1914 was *Cinderella*, which played from
Boxing Day 'until further notice' at the Theatre Royal. Ticket prices
ranged from 6d to 3s.

CHAPTER TWO

1915 – Deepening Conflict

At the beginning of January, Mr S. M. J. Woods (Sammy), the well-known Somerset cricketer and old Cantab, volunteered for the army and was granted a lieutenant's commission in the Somerset Regiment.

Kitchener's recruitment poster, 'Your country needs you!' A huge recruitment campaign encouraged young men to join-up. By January 1915, almost 1,000,000 men had enlisted. Pals battalions encouraged many to enlist and they ultimately provided enough men for three battalions.

The Great Resolution. The advert was featured in newspapers of 1 January 1915 and encouraged men to enlist. The slogan read: 'I will be a man and enlist today!' Men were urged to report to their nearest recruiting office as soon as possible.

Driving a lorry through the water outside Stothert and Pitt's during January 1915. Staff of the company had to be conveyed to and from work in carts due to the heavy flooding. The tram service to Twerton and Bathford was temporarily broken and Messrs Collins' flour mill was compelled to close for the day.

On 4 January, Bath suffered severe flooding after heavy rain and melting snow. Low lying areas of Bath were inundated and some businesses suffered flooding of their cellars and basements. The tram service at Twerton and Bathford was temporarily broken and employees of Messrs Stothert and Pitt had to be conveyed along the

British and Belgian soldiers who were patients at the Royal Mineral Water Hospital were invited to the matinee performance of the city's pantomime Cinderella on Wednesday 6 January 1915.

Royal Mineral Water Hospital, Bath, from the garden.

flooded road in carts. Messrs Collins' flour mill had to close for a day because of the water and at Messrs Cook's factory at Twerton, the water reached a gas engine closing down part of the works.

British and Belgian soldiers who were patients at the Royal Mineral Water Hospital were invited to the matinee performance of the city's pantomime *Cinderella* on Wednesday 6 January. The soldiers who attended numbered thirty, being nineteen Belgians and eleven British, who occupied the first two rows of the pit. They were said to have greatly enjoyed the performance. Miss Anna Deirdre, who had invited them, also distributed cigarettes to the soldiers, which were much appreciated.

Mrs W. E. Hardy of York Villa stated that she would be very much obliged if any ladies in Bath would assist her in sending to each employee of the Bath Electric Tramways, serving at the front (about eighty-five men) a woollen helmet and muffler. She said that such gifts would be very much appreciated by the men and should be forwarded to her at York Villa.

A letter dated 6 January from Sapper N. V. H. Symons, a son of the headmaster at King Edward School, Bath, stated that the 1st Wessex Engineers, who were made up almost entirely of men from Bath and Weston-Super-Mare, were now in the firing line. He wrote that they had marched from their farm billet on Tuesday 5 January, from 8.30 am to 3 pm. He said that the marching was so severe that by the time they reached their destination only six out of the forty men in Sapper Symon's unit were left. He finished his letter with:

> *Today, we have covered 10 or 11 miles of cobbles and most of us are absolutely dead lame. We are now in the thick of it and shells are literally bursting all around us.*

On 9 January, the *Bath Chronicle* reported that the Mayor of Bath had received a letter from Major Lubbock, the officer commanding 'A' Squadron of the North Somerset Yeomanry. It was headed 'Somewhere in France' and read:

> *My dear Mr. Mayor, I wish to write you these few lines to express on behalf of the Bath Squadron North Somerset Yeomanry, our sincere gratitude for the many and varied gifts of chocolates, tobacco, cigarettes and warm clothing which from time to time have arrived*

for the non-commissioned officers and men who are on active service here in France, and to ask if you will be so good as to convey to the donors our heart-felt thanks and appreciation of their kind thoughts. I think that I may say our Christmas dinner, held within earshot of the guns at a Brasserie Brewery nearby, was an unqualified success and heartily enjoyed by all present. The menu was as follows:-

Geese a la Francaise, with plenty of stuffing, apple sauce and vegetables, followed by good old English plum pudding, cheese and dessert, with beer provided by our kindly host, Monsieur Lefebvre, owner of the brewery, to wash down this truly seasonable repast. I may say that the toast of our generous benefactors, coupled with your name, was drunk and received amid rousing cheers and the unanimous wish was expressed that our friends from Bath and the West Country could have been present to learn for themselves how much their kind gifts had been appreciated. Wishing you, sir, from all and every one of us, a happy and a very prosperous New Year. I remain, yours truly, Geoffrey Lubbock, Major, Officer commanding A Squadron, N.S.Y.

P.S. I forgot to mention that on Christmas Eve some of our men visited several of the farms nearby and treated them to an excellent selection of carols. The singing was of a very high order as I can testify to personally being billeted at one of the farms myself.

After playing a match with Bath XV on Saturday 16 January, the Canadian rugby team were entertained at Red House. Their captain, Mr L. M. Speirs, who had previously dislocated a shoulder, was able to re-join the company. Mr Arthur Taylor, chairman of the Bath Football Club, proposed the health of His Majesty's Forces with special reference to the Canadian contingent and their visitors of that day. He said that not only the club but the city was delighted to see the Canadian team and he hoped that after the war they would be able to visit again.

Mr Speirs replied that the hospitality they had received from the moment they got off the train at Bath had been absolutely extraordinary. He continued that if the men returned from the war then they would certainly play another match in Bath. This brought much applause. In response to their captain's call, the Canadians drank to the health of the Bath Club.

After dinner, the Canadians went to see a performance of the pantomime where the actors made allusions to their presence in song and joke. The visitors enjoyed the show very much and returned to their camp on Salisbury Plain on Sunday evening.

On Saturday 23 January, the *Bath Chronicle* told the tale of a Bath motor driver and his son meeting unexpectedly at the Front. It was said that there was no better known member of the Bath Tramways Company's uniformed staff than driver James Padfield. He was one of the original motormen of the electric trams but had, more recently, been a driver of torpedo charabancs. He was one of the first to enlist in the war and on 12 October joined the Army Service Corps, Motor Transport Section. Eight days later he left Britain for the Continent. His only son, Herbert, was already a member of the Wessex Territorial Royal Engineers, having joined on 2 October 1914. Just before Christmas 1914, he landed in the country where his father had been on active service for two months.

James Padfield wrote back to his wife telling her that he had bumped into their son. In his letter he wrote:

I met Herbert this morning. We were returning from the railhead and got held up for some troops to pass. It was the remainder of those that Herbert was with. I asked them if they had come from Winchester and they replied 'Yes'. I knew I should find him because we passed three sections of the Wessex the day before, and that night I spent three hours in the rain, mud and dark trying to find him but I failed. Had I known it, they had been, since Christmas Day, within about five miles of the village we stop at. There were many among those we passed the first day knew me and they shouted 'Good Old Bath.' I recognised more from Weston-Super-Mare, the lot Herbert was with. I hope to see him again tomorrow as I hope they will be billeted on our road, where we deliver to the 11th Hussars.

In a later letter, Mr Padfield said that his son looked 'quite well and jolly.'

Sapper Herbert Padfield also wrote home to his mother telling of his meeting with his father. In his letter, he wrote:

We were passing through an A.S.C. base on the 6th and I saw dad with his lorry. He was stopped, so I dropped out of the ranks and spoke to him but as I had to catch up with the rest, I hadn't time to tell him or hear very much but he is all right and looks as in good health as he ever did. We are now in the danger zone. The artillery is within half a mile of our billets. The Germans are dropping shells all round here but not doing any damage.

On Saturday 20 February, the *Bath Chronicle* published a story under the headline 'A Battlefield Souvenir.' It read:

A young Somerset soldier called at our offices this week with a gruesome battlefield souvenir. It was the military cap of a Bath man, serving with the Somersets at the front, who was killed while taking part in a gallant charge undertaken to drive the Germans out of certain trenches. The cap contains five distinct bullet holes.

The young soldier who brought the mournful exhibit was himself badly wounded in the charge. A bullet entered one of the fingers on his left hand, passed out by the palm of his hand, struck the magazine of his rifle and was deflected into his left arm. Another bullet damaged his left ankle and he also received a piece of a shrapnel shell in the right shoulder. The injury to the left hand and arm is, unfortunately, very serious. Yet the young soldier, who modestly declined to give his name, made no fuss about it and laughingly remarked that he was having the bullet, which damaged his arm, mounted as a brooch.

He was disinclined to talk about his experiences but he mentioned that he was at the front for three months and took part in seven bayonet charges. His company of the Somersets, B Company, witnessed the famous charge of the 9th Lancers. On that occasion, it will be remembered, the Germans threw down their arms as the Lancers bore down upon them, with the result our men passed through them without intentionally hurting a man. Thereupon the Germans picked up their rifles again and fired at the horsemen, who had their backs to them. 'You should have seen the Lancers wheel round and go for them,' said the young soldier with enthusiasm. 'They went through them once, came back again, and through them again. Then there was scarcely a German left alive. I was one of the party who buried hundreds of them.'

On 30 January, a letter was published in the *Bath Chronicle* from

Sergeant Ben Hurst, who had regularly written to the newspaper from France. It read:

We are still in the same spot but are now getting more excitement, in the shape of 'trips to the trenches' and the whole business is much more interesting. I have been up on several occasions and must say that although it's not exactly like going to the Palace, there is a certain fascination about it. We go up at night in small parties, the size of which varies according to the work to be done, and return in the morning before daylight. I cannot describe our work to you but it consists mostly in improvements. The trenches around here are not quite like the pictures in the illustrated papers (which show them arranged in miniature 'Hotel Cecil' fashion) and in consequence our work is much harder than in ordinary 'circs'. Up to the present, I've done no dashing bayonet charging, or, as far as I can gather, killed any Germans but then neither have they killed me, so, on counting up, the result is a 'dead heat'. I have blinded a few rounds into the German trenches but, of course, being at night, it was too dark to see anything and the dirty beggars would not signal the results of the shots. So far, the Germans have never charged a trench in which the 1st Wessex boys have been at work. They take a delight in wasting good ammunition at us (until now with absolutely no result)

but they always stay on their own dust heap, and never venture across to us, and as a rule it's not far to come. I can tell you that I've carefully thought the matter over and think it must be the reputation that the Somerset men have got, that is the cause of it. The German spies (there are millions) find out we are going up to work in the trenches and send word to their 'confreres' (good word, it's French; I always throw one or two in my letters now) and they say we had better leave them alone tonight, or there will be trouble, and the result is that we've had no dirty

Sergeant E. Evans, of the North Somerset Yeomanry, who was mentioned in dispatches for gallant and distinguished service in the field. Sergeant Evans resided at South Lodge, North Parade Bridge, Bath. Published in the Bath Chronicle of Saturday 20 February 1915.

work at all. Really we have been exceptionally lucky and plenty of the infantry have been wounded in the trenches we work in, and if you listen to the tales of some of the men who have been up, it's a wonder they have not been blown completely back to Bath from here. Everyone is pretty fit when one considers the delightful spring weather.

In February, Sergeant A. E. Winstone of the South Midland RE wrote to his cousin in Bath about his experiences at the front. The letter read:

Whilst I was in the trenches last time, I saw someone with a lighted cigarette in his mouth. I thought it was a sapper and shouted to him to put it out, but he did not seem to take any notice, so I shouted: 'If you do not put that light out, I will put yours out.' No notice was taken, and as I thought it was endangering the troops, for a light like that shows up very much, I picked up a handful of wet mud and let go. Who do you think it was? It was an officer of ours, and one of the best, too. I was sorry when I found out who I had hit, as he is as good a man as we could be under, but we could not help laughing at the time.

Private Jack Holbrook of the 4th Somerset Light Infantry, who wrote home while stationed in India in 1915. He said: 'It is just like being on Salisbury Plain here. We are right out in the open country and live in bungalows – 100 men in each.' Private Holbrook was the son of Mr and Mrs J. W. Holbrook, of Stratton-on-the-Fosse, and prior to the war had worked at Messrs Stothert and Pitt's.

On 6 March, the *Bath Chronicle* reported that more troops were on the way to Bath. The headline read 'Additional thousand men arrive next week.' the story read:

Arrangements are almost complete for the quartering in Bath of additional troops, and the men, numbering about a thousand, belonging to the Hampshires, will arrive during the early part of next week. A large proportion of the soldiers will be billeted in houses in the Bathwick district and the County Skating Rink has also been requisitioned for the purpose and here it is proposed to accommodate between 400 and 450 men. The houses which are to receive the men are now being prepared for their new occupants.

In May it was decided, by the committee set up in the city to aid prisoners-of-war, that a weekly parcel of food should be sent to all men belonging to the city and adjoining parishes who were known to be interned overseas. It was decided that an appeal would be issued for funds while the honorary secretary, Mr Van Sommer, requested the names and addresses of Bath men interned in Germany.

On the afternoon of 7 May, the *Lusitania* was torpedoed by a German U-boat 11 miles off the southern coast of Ireland. A total of 1,195 lost their lives. By firing on a non-military ship, the Germans had breached international laws. There was such a protest in the United States that it eventually influenced America to enter the war in 1917.

On Saturday 8 May, the Mayor of Bath, at the conclusion of a

RMS Lusitania. On the afternoon of 7 May 1915, the Lusitania was torpedoed leading to a loss of 1,195 lives. The event eventually influenced America to enter the war in 1917.

concert at the Pump Room, referred to the sinking of the *Lusitania*. 'All that day,' he said, 'the dark cloud of sorrow had been hanging over all those who had heard the sad tidings. Indeed, that cloud had first enfolded them on the evening of the previous day but, at first, it had been hoped, that only the ship had been lost and those aboard her had been saved. But in the morning they had learned that many lives had been sacrificed – the lives, too, of non-combatants including women and little children who were not to be justly regarded as liable to those grave risks which warriors had to face.'

A meeting of the Bath Rural District Council was held at the Poor Law Offices on Wednesday 19 May. The clerk read out a letter from Mr. F. B. Beauchamp of Woodborough House. It read:

> *In view of the shortness of labour available for agriculture, in consequence of the war, is it possible to arrange during harvest and seeding time, that all men now employed on the roads by the Council should be at the disposal of the various farmers if so required? I know that a large amount of work is essential but I think you will agree with me that there is a good deal of time spent on the roads in keeping them clean and the sides tidy etc., which is not so important as growing food supplies for our country, especially in view of the rapidly increasing cost of living. I am asking the chairman of the County Council to take this matter up and bring it before the County Works Committee as, owing to being called up for military duties, I shall not be able to attend the next meeting.*

Mr Andrews, councillor, thought that they should deal with the matter as the necessity arose and Mr Stride, chairman, said that it was a very important matter and the same question had been asked of them at the last harvest-time. Previously, the council had thought it was not advisable as it would cause friction but now, with altered circumstances, agreed with the suggestion. Mr Stride moved that the letter be referred to the Finance and General Purposes Committee. Mr Hooper, councillor for Batheaston, stating that if they took their men off the roads, it might be prejudicial to health. He felt there would be great jealousy amongst the agriculturists because 'one man might get a man from the roads and another man might not'.

Mr Stride's motion was carried.

The interior of the Grand Pump Room. During Christmas 1915, the Pump Room hosted a lavish party for children whose fathers were away fighting in the war. The event had its own Santa Claus, who handed out crackers to the excited children.

In July, the mayor received a letter enclosing cash from the headmistress of South Twerton school. The cash, a total of £6 10s, was raised by the infants attending the school giving concerts. The cash was added to the equipment fund for the Bath War Hospital. On the previous Sunday afternoon at Sydney Gardens, over £50 had been collected for the fund.

In early September, a letter from Frank Stell from Weston was published in the local paper. He was the third officer on board a steamship transporting troops to the Dardanelles. His ship took soldiers to the first landing on the Gallipoli Peninsula. Writing of his second trip to Sulva Bay, he wrote:

We have arrived safely back to Alexandria after an exciting and adventurous trip. We were under a constant rain of shell fire for ten days. It was not a bad sport but I'm in no hurry for a repetition of the experience. It is a marvel to me how we escaped unhit. They used to commence operations by shelling the ships in the bay at 6 am. There were about a dozen of us and we would all heave up and cruise around until they had finished. The next performance would start at 10 am and last until 11.30 am. Then again at 1.30 pm until

4 pm. Then they would have a rest and start again at 6 pm until 8 pm. just to liven things up, a couple of aeroplanes would circle over us and drop bombs. One night they dropped one in the camp and killed sixty men, fortunately they missed the ships every time.

The way our fellows are fighting is absolutely marvellous and one cannot but feel proud of being a Britisher. In the landing we have just left, we have lost a terrible amount. Out of one body of 3,000, only 900 are left. People at home cannot imagine the difficulties our fellows have to meet and yet when you meet them they seem unaware that they are doing anything out of the ordinary. We had on board us about a hundred of the Naval Division. They have been cut up badly. Three times they have been rebanded. Poor beggars, I did feel sorry for them. They were covered in grime from head to toe, for they had been unable to get a wash for days. Some of them only had the clothes they stood up in and pitiful objects they looked. However, we did our best for them as far as we were able, with regard to food, water and soap.

I did not feel any too comfortable when the first shell came flying over the bridge and they can say what they like about the shell having arrived before the noise is heard and it is useless to duck until the danger is over. I ducked any rate and so did the naval and military officers we had with us and they were accustomed to it. It is no pleasant experience being on an open unprotected bridge. You hear a whiz and then a bang and a cloud of spray near you. Then you know the Turks have scored another miss. Now our fellows are firmly established on the Peninsula, they will never drive them out.

We had a fine passage down here; quite uneventful, although submarines are kicking about somewhere, and we had to keep a sharp look-out for them.

On Wednesday 15 September, at 3 o'clock, an army airman flying over Combe Down narrowly avoided a serious accident. Three aviators had set out from Salisbury Plain in three separate machines intending to fly to another destination in Wiltshire. The sky became overcast and the weather so hazy that they lost their course with all of them eventually passing over the outskirts of Bath. One of the trio, flying a large biplane, became separated from the others and was passing over a field adjoining the Statutory Hospital at Claverton Down when his engine unexpectedly stopped. He managed to make a good landing but before the speed of his biplane could be checked, he ploughed into a wall, which resulted in his propeller and three stays being broken. Luckily, the airman escaped unhurt.

Many rushed to his assistance and he explained that although he was only flying at a height of about 1,000 feet when his engine packed in, he could not see where he was going. His destination had been Netheravon.

PATRIOTIC NEWTON FAMILY.

FIVE BROTHERS WITH THE COLOURS.

Mrs. Perry, a widow resident in the parish of Newton St. Loe, is the mother of seven sons, no fewer than five of whom are serving now with the Colours. As an incentive towards recruiting, and a witness of the mother's splendid sacrifice to her country, the circumstances, as an esteemed correspondent points out, are certainly worthy of the widest publicity. Below we reproduce photos of the mother and her gallant soldier sons.

Private R. J. PERRY,
Duke of Cornwall's L.I.

Mrs. PERRY, the Mother.

Driver C. P. PERRY,
Royal Horse Artillery.

Driver A. S. PERRY,
Royal Field Artillery.

Private R. A. PERRY,
6th Somerset L.I.

Private C. T. PERRY,
Royal Marine L.I.

The Bath Chronicle of Saturday 5 October 1915 showed a patriotic Newton family under the headline: 'Five Brothers with the Colours.' The article read: 'Mrs Perry, a widow resident in the parish of Newton St Loe, is the mother of seven sons, no fewer than five of whom are now serving with the Colours. As an incentive towards recruiting, and a witness of the mother's splendid sacrifice to her country, the circumstances, as an esteemed foreign correspondent points out, are certainly worthy of the widest publicity.'

In October, it was announced that the War Office had accepted the services of the committee, set up by the mayor, to run the Bath War Hospital and that they approved of the scheme of management suggested to them. The War Office appointed Dr G. A. Bannatyne as commandant of the hospital. A meeting was held on the 27 October at the Guildhall in support of the work and it was requested that all people interested in the care of the wounded soldiers should attend.

On Tuesday 5 October, Mrs Browne of 12 Park Road, Bath, received news that her younger son, Major F. M. Browne, DSO RE, had died of

FOR KING AND COUNTRY.

The late Captain H. L. SKRINE.

6th Somersets.

Captain G. TRAVERS BIGGS.

1st Glamorgan A.T.C., R.E.,
son of Mrs. Biggs, Greenway Lodge, Bath.

Lieut. G. H. NEVILLE.

1st Somerset L.I.
formerly recruiting sergeant in Bath.

2nd-Lieut. LIONEL LOCK.

5th Batt. Northumberland Fusiliers,
son of Mr. T. Lock, of Sybil Lodge,
Oldfield Park.

Major TAYLOR.

R.A.M.C.,
son of the late Mr. J. D. Taylor, of
Blair Athole, Bath.

2nd-Lieut. A. E. TAYLOR.

Army Service Corps,
son of the late Mr. J. D. Taylor, of
Blair Athole.

The Bath Chronicle of Saturday 5 October 1915 showed a display of photos of soldiers under the heading 'For King and Country'. This was a regular feature in the newspaper throughout the war.

Captain Cyril Shannon, whose death was reported in the Bath Chronicle of Saturday 5 October 1915. Captain Shannon was a member of the Royal Engineers. He was killed in action between 1 and 4 October on the Western Front. Before being sent to France at the outbreak of war, he had served three years in Hong Kong where he had studied the Japanese language. He was told by his examiner that he could speak Japanese better than any other living Englishman.

For king and country. Photos of members of the armed forces involved in the conflict overseas appeared in the Bath Chronicle of 9 October 1915.

Private Bert Lewis. Bert Lewis was formerly captain of the Walcot rugby team and afterwards, a three-quarter for Bath. He was at the side of Private Tom West when West was struck down by a German bullet.

wounds on 1 October. Major Browne was well-known in Bath and had seen action overseas before the beginning of the First World War. In 1900, he had served in China and was present at the relief of Tientsin and Peking, where he was severely wounded. He had joined the Royal Engineers in 1892. Major Browne was mentioned in dispatches and had received his DSO in February.

On Saturday 9 October, the *Bath Chronicle* announced that Tom West, a well-known Bath rugby footballer, had died in action. His parents, Mr and Mrs Walter West of 17 Stuart Place, Twerton, received news on the previous Saturday night that he had been killed in action on Wednesday 29 September. Rifleman Tom West had served with 'A' Company of the 10th Battalion King's Royal Rifle Corps. The officer who wrote to tell his parents of his death said that he died instantaneously and remarked: 'He was a good soldier, a kind friend, faithful in his duty and will be missed by all.'

Enclosed with the note was a letter that Rifleman West had written to his mother but had not lived long enough to post. It began with the message:

I may not have the opportunity of writing to you for a little while, so you must not worry if you don't hear from me. I shall be quite all right. We are keeping in good condition.

Tom West first played rugby for the Oldfield Park Club before joining the Bath XV.

The *Chronicle* reported:

An incident at the Cup Final in March 1907 will never be forgotten by those who witnessed the match. It was the first season the cup had been put up and there was a splendid struggle with Bridgwater Albion. Towards the end of the game, West seemed to be winning it for Bath. Dick Meister (now also a soldier), at centre, came away and passed to Tom West on the right wing. West seemed certain to score, for his speed would have enabled him to outdistance two opponents who tried to cut him off. But at the critical moment, he made the mistake of trying to double through and dodge. He was tackled and the glorious chance went. In extra time, Bath lost by a goal.

West also made several appearances for Somerset. But in 1908, he forsook amateur rugby for the Northern Union, being secured by Rochdale Hornets. With them he played finely and assisted in winning the Northern Union Cup for his team. He held a good position in the Corporation Electricity Works at Rochdale. This he threw up, and also his football, to join the Army last autumn, when he enlisted in the Rifle Corps. He was in Bath at Christmas on leave and went to the front with his regiment only a short time ago.

When at Aldershot, he met on the parade ground an old Bath football and running pal who had also enlisted in the same battalion. This was Bert Lewis, formerly captain of the Walcot rugby team and afterwards, a three-quarter for Bath. He was in their quartette in the Cup Final to which allusion has been made. It was a delightful surprise to the men to find themselves comrades and they had been together ever since. Lewis was at Tom's side when he was struck down by a German bullet and has written home to tell of West's glorious death.

During November, a boy reported to the local police that he had seen two strangers, who he took to be German spies. He said that they conversed at night by use of their motor lamps and spoke in an unfamiliar language.

The police spent a considerable time investigating the matter before deciding that the men were merely government officials who had experienced trouble with their motor lamps. The visit from the officials was due to a foot and mouth outbreak and they were in Bath to inspect cattle.

At the beginning of November, a letter was received by the Bath

Prisoners of War Help Committee. It was sent by Lance-Corporal Payton, 2nd Welsh, who was interned near Posen. The letter read:

I received your parcel in good condition and thank you for same. I am working on a farm, We are a party of twenty soldiers all from different regiments. We commence work at 5.30 am and we have half an hour for breakfast and an hour and a half for dinner, half an hour for tea at 4 pm and finish at 8 pm to receive threepence a day. I am in good health; it is very healthy here this time of the year but it is very cold in winter. If you have such an article as a knitted jacket, scarf or knitted cap that you could send me, I should be much obliged to you for same. What you sent me in your parcel were just the things I needed. We are in German Poland; we all stop in the one house and are locked in all night. The food is better here than in camp. We are allowed to write two letters a month and a postcard every week. I do not mind the work so much but I long for freedom once again. We cannot go through life without a certain amount of self-sacrifice. We have some prayer books, so we have Divine service on Sunday. I conduct the service.

As a boy, Lance-Corporal Payton was educated at the Somerset Industrial School in Bath.

In November, Mrs Ham of 30 Burnham Road, Twerton, brought an object to the offices of the *Bath Chronicle* which was a war souvenir in the form of a model coal scuttle. It had been made from a French

'75' shell and had been sent to her by her eldest son, George, who had enlisted at the beginning of the war in the Royal Horse Artillery. He had been at the Front for ten months. George was serving with the North Somerset Yeomanry and had been in France for five months.

Private Frank Cutting of the 1st Battalion Welsh Regiment. Private Frank Cutting, who was reported missing in action and then found to be alive but injured in a German Field Hospital. The story appeared in newspapers during December 1915.

The *Bath Chronicle* of Saturday 11 December carried the story of a missing soldier. It read:

Mr and Mrs John Cutting, of 2 George Street, Bath, on Saturday, received definite news as to the whereabouts of their son, Private Frank Cutting, of the 1st Battalion Welsh Regiment. Frank, who is 19 years of age and was formerly in the service of Messrs. E Peacock and Sons, Union Street, enlisted last February, and was sent to the front during the summer. Two months and three weeks ago, his parents received official intelligence – a War Office notification – that their son was missing. Mr. Cutting was formerly a cab proprietor in Bath, as were many of his family, but of late he has been a wheel-chairman, standing at Laura Place. A lady visitor, whom he has taken about in his chair, when in Bath a little while ago, undertook to do everything in her power to ascertain news of the missing soldier. The lady is Miss Morris of Chesham Place, Brighton who has brothers, officers in the Army. It was from her that a letter arrived from 2 Grove Street, this morning, and it enclosed a communication from the British Red Cross and Order of St John

On the right of the photo is Mr R. P. Guy of Bath, who had been acting as a flying instructor with the Russian Army, a post for which he was chosen from amongst several hundred applicants. Mr Guy was an old Technical School boy and was the son of Mr Percy Guy who, for many years, was connected with Messrs Evans and Owen.

Meals in the trenches usually consisted of bully beef but behind the lines the food could be quite varied as shown here on Christmas Day 1915. A tray of plump chickens has been prepared for the men as they are called to the cookhouse by a bugler of the Army Veterinary Corps.

inquiry agency at Geneva stating that Frank Cutting, 33079, 1st Welsh Regiment, was in the German list of prisoners dated November 13. He was stated to be wounded in the back, right arm and right foot and to be an inmate of the Feldlazaret Phalempire. Feldlazaret means Field Hospital and the communication states that prisoners only stay there for a short time, so it is unadvisable to send parcels to that address. Miss Morris promises to ascertain his subsequent address, if possible, but suggests that the parents should get in touch with the Bath Prisoners' Aid Committee. This the mother has already done. Private Cutting joined the Welsh Regiment because his sister's husband, who worked in South Wales, had done so, and his brother-in-law is now in France. Private Cutting was a boy at Bathwick School and a member of Miss Awdry's Bible Class. His parents are extremely glad to obtain the news and are hoping that their boy may recover and be restored to them.

An article about Christmas entertainment in Bath appeared in the *Western Daily Press* of Wednesday 29th December. It read:

Concerts of the stereotyped order are by no means the sole entertainment provided now at the Bath Pump Room or, to be strictly correct, in the Roman Annexe, for the recent renovated Grand Pump Room is used solely for the accommodation of water drinkers. Perhaps the most seasonable event happened yesterday, when the afternoon and early evening were devoted to a children's party. Father Christmas, in time-honoured garb, handed crackers to the company and tables were set apart for jolly juvenile tea parties. Then came 'Punch and Judy' and for once the celebrated orchestra was put completely in the shade, in the opinion of the delighted youngsters. Pre-Yuletide specialities included an afternoon devoted to 'Music of One Hundred Years Ago,' which the enterprising conductor, Mr. G. B. Robinson had unearthed in the Pump Room band's library.

With an excellent Christmas pantomime, 'Aladdin', just launched on what promises to be a popular month's course at the Theatre Royal, and other attractions, there is no lack of seasonable entertainment and amusement at Bath just now.

Meanwhile, at the Vaudeville Electric Theatre in Westgate Street, the special Christmas programme included, *Nan in Fairyland* and was due to show from Monday until Wednesday. It was followed by *Cinderella*, which starred Mary Pickford.

An advert for the Christmas pantomime of 1915, Aladdin. The show featured Mabel Hind as Aladdin, Fred Hutchings as Abanazar and the Brothers Valdo as the policemen.

CHAPTER THREE

1916 – Realization

Compulsory enlistment for men between the ages of 18 and 41 was introduced for single men and childless widowers. However, essential war workers, clergymen, the physically unfit and approved conscientious objectors were exempt. The upper age was later raised to 51.

In January, Major Sir Charles Hunter, MP for Bath, announced that he was amongst the members of parliament who had decided to give up their salaries in connection with the wartime economy movement.

On Wednesday 12 January, Private Edward Dickinson of the 4th Battalion Tyneside Scottish appeared before magistrates at the Bath City Police Court. He was charged with being absent from his regiment since 3 January.

PC Hitchcock told the court that he approached Dickinson near the railway station and told him that he was making enquiries about a prisoner who had escaped from military police in Warminster who had travelled to Bath without a ticket. Dickinson refused to give the constable any information and

A recruitment poster stating 'Women of Britain say Go!' In January 1916, the Military Service Bill was introduced forcing the conscription of single men between the ages of 18 and 41. In May, conscription was extended to married men also.

while being escorted to the police station, offered to fight the policeman several times.

In court, Dickinson said he had planned to return to camp and the magistrate said he would be taken there under escort.

PC Hitchcock was recommended for a reward of 5s.

| PALACE THEATRE, BATH. | **Next Week.** The Famous SIX BROTHERS LUCK present their First Musical Comedy Burlesque ENTITLED "SOME TREASURE." IN FIVE SCENES. FULL CASTE OF LONDON STAR ARTISTES. |

The famous Six Brothers Luck presented their first musical comedy burlesque, Some Treasure at the Palace Theatre towards the end of January 1916.

On Tuesday 18 January, there was a rush for seats at the Assembly Rooms when Madame Clara Butt made her annual visit to the city. The large ballroom was packed with people with overflow chairs in the Octagon. Madame Butt received a magnificent reception and was enthusiastically recalled after each performance. At one encore, she sang *Sweetest Flower*, which attracted much applause.

In the Pump Room Concert Hall in the afternoon and evening, Mr

Clara Butt with her husband Kennerley Rumford. Clara Butt visited Bath on 18 January 1916 and received a magnificent reception. She was famous for being a recitalist and concert singer and sang for many service charities during the First World War.

Arthur B. Malden gave travel talks about Russia. Despite there being counter attractions, his talks still received large audiences.

Meanwhile, at the Theatre Royal, the Bath pantomime *Aladdin*, starring Miss Mabel Hind, came to an end on Saturday 22 January and was replaced with *The Rage of London: Potash and Perlmutter*. Commencing at the Palace was *The Four Diving Norins*, described as 'The World's Greatest Diving Act', while over at the Vaudeville Electric Theatre in Westgate Street, they were previewing *Jim the Penman*, a detective story.

The story of a landslide at Batheaston appeared in the Bath Chronicle of Saturday 26 January 1918. The story read: 'Exactly 9am on Monday, there was an extensive fall of retaining wall, and the ground behind it, from the London Road just on the Batheaston side of Clarence Gardens, Batheaston. The wall has gone for a length of 40 yards and, as it stood 16ft high from the ground, the quantity of masonry that fell was large, while many tons of earth went with its support. The cause of the landslide is believed to be waterlogging. The subsidence was hastened by the snow, thaw and rain of last week.'

During January Mark Parker, of the Viaduct Hotel, Monkton Combe, appeared at the Weston County Police Court for failing to keep a register in accordance with the Amendment Order of the Aliens Restriction Act 1915. He was told that he must present each visitor with a form to fill in and then record them in a register. Even though he had had no aliens staying with him, he was fined £25 in a case that baffled the defence. His solicitor, Mr Glover, gave notice of appeal against the conviction.

On Saturday 5 February, the *Bath Chronicle* carried the news 'Springbok in Bath'. The story read:

> *Several Bathonians were greatly pleased to receive a surprise visit from Mr. P. Braine, one of the South African Rugby football team, which came to England in 1912 and played in Bath. Mr. Braine has come to England to take a commission in the British Army. He has already done some fighting for the flag, having gone through the German South-West African campaign. Mr. Braine, who is none the worse for that experience, and looks extremely fit, gave interesting news of many of the Springbok team, several of whom have also been fighting for the Empire against the Germans. They all look back and still speak with pleasure of the happy time they spent in Bath.*

An advert for the last night of the pantomime, Aladdin, at the Theatre Royal on Saturday 22 January 1916. The part of Aladdin was played by Miss Lillie Lassah and the show featured popular songs of the day.

The *Western Daily Press* of 10 February reported that Mr and Mrs Rudyard Kipling had been staying in the city. They had visited once before in the previous spring.

Members of the Somerset Regiment. The photo shows the 5th Battalion of the Somerset Light Infantry TF at camp. A bugler is sitting cross-legged at the front of the group.

Bath War Hospital Ward No 6. Troops, staff and nurses pose for the camera. The hospital was located at Combe Park.

The *Bath Chronicle* of Saturday 4 March reported that the film *The Four Feathers* was showing at the Vaudeville Picture Theatre. The film version of Captain A. E. W. Mason's military novel was of special interest to Bathonians because it was the production of a local enterprise – the Lucoque Film Producing Company of Bath, London and New York. The film dealt with the fear of being accused of cowardice and the white feathers issued by women to men who were not enlisted in the forces.

On the afternoon of Monday 3 April, donors to the Bath War Hospital were invited to attend an inspection of its wards. Anyone who paid a shilling to enter was welcome and the money taken went towards

The grounds of Bath War Hospital. Recovering soldiers can be seen exercising in the grounds of the hospital. The specially prepared huts to house the wounded can be seen in the background.

the fund. Altogether, over 1,100 people passed through the doors and a total of £52 7s was collected.

On Thursday 6 April, the 600 Company ASC (Motor Transport), who had trained in Bath for several months, left the city at 1 o'clock for a foreign destination. Their final roll-call took place in Dartington Street and on its completion their commanding officer, Captain Nash Wortham, called for three cheers for the people of Bath. The response of the troops showed that they were in complete appreciation of the many kindnesses they had received from the citizens. Shortly afterwards the men marched to their lorries which then set off along Pulteney Street while cheering and waving handkerchiefs from the windows. The soldiers were in excellent spirits and made no secret that they were glad of the opportunity to 'do their bit'.

The mayor's intention was to attend their departure and to give a farewell speech but the departure was so hurried that there was no time for a ceremony. Instead the mayor wrote a letter to Captain Nash Wortham. It read:

A postcard showing the smiling faces of members of the navy and army working together. The caption reads: 'You never know what you can do till you try.'

YOU NEVER KNOW WHAT YOU CAN DO 'TILL YOU TRY.

Dear Captain Wortham, Many thanks for your kind letter expressing the thanks of the officers, N.C.O.s and men of the 600 M.T. A.C.S. to the citizens of Bath for the kindness shown to them during their stay in the city. I should have very much liked to come down, taken a brief farewell, and wished God-speed to the men of your Company on their leaving for active service, but I quite understand the rush of the moment and that it is impossible for you to make arrangements. But I cannot allow you and your Company to leave Bath, where you have been stationed for about six months, without thanking you all for having upheld the record established by all the regiments which we have had the good fortune to have had quartered in the city.

Your part in the great venture will not be without its perils and the citizens of Bath earnestly hope and pray that you will be protected in all circumstances. We wish you God-speed and that you may soon return in health and strength, the victory won, to the homes you are now going forth to defend. With all good wishes.

Believe me, yours faithfully, H. T. Hatt, Mayor.

At the beginning of April, news was received from members of the Abbey Football Club who were occupying a line of trenches in

On Tuesday 11 April 1916, the Pump Room Orchestra gave a concert at Prior Park for the Canadian soldiers stationed in Bath. A feature of the programme was the fantasia The Allies in Camp, with Miss Hilda Blake as vocalist.

Flanders. Privates Moon and Howard, of the Somerset Light Infantry, had both been wounded but were progressing well. Private Hooper was convalescing after an illness. The Church Lad's Brigade Company deeply regretted the loss of Private Bush, who was killed in action.

On Tuesday 11 April, the Pump Room Orchestra gave a concert at Prior Park for the Canadian soldiers stationed in Bath. A feature of the programme was the fantasia *The Allies in Camp*, with Miss Hilda Blake as the vocalist.

The *Western Daily Press* of Thursday 20 April ran a story about Easter in Bath. It read:

> *Bath is exceedingly full of visitors for Easter, notwithstanding the dreary weather that is being experienced, and the hotels are crowded. The management of the Pump Room and the Roman Promenade has prepared a special series of attractions for the holiday time. On Bank Holiday, Miss Nora Reed is the special soloist at the afternoon and evening concerts and she sings again on Tuesday and Wednesday afternoons.*
>
> *On Saturday 29th, Madame Sarah Bernhardt is making her first appearance in Bath, giving a matinee performance at the Theatre Royal.*
>
> *Outdoor amusements will not be entirely omitted as the New Zealand Expeditionary Force XV, from Essex, after playing Swansea on Saturday, meet a Bath team at the Recreation Ground on Easter Thursday afternoon. Rugby football has been at a standstill since the war but with the help of Canadian players from Prior Park, the Bath Club is putting into the field a strong side. The Mayor is welcoming the New Zealanders and presiding at a dinner to them after the game.*

During May, the first batch of prosecutions under the new Lighting Order were heard at the Bath City Police Court in the presence of the mayor, Alderman T. F. Plowman and Alderman E. E. Phillips:

> *Arthur Goodrop, of 44 Southgate Street, for not obscuring or shading lights on his shop. Sergeant Sanders stated the facts and the offence was admitted.*
>
> *Walter Gayner, of 23 Southgate Street, pleaded guilty to a similar offence. The defendant stated, 'I've done my best. I can do no more.'*

Mrs Salome Miller, of 4 Southgate Street, was charged with a similar offence. PC Davis gave evidence and stated that when he pointed out the excessive light, Mrs Miller said to him, 'You are worse here than you are in London or on the East Coast. Are you trying to drive people mad, or what are you trying to do?' It was said that there were dark blinds in the shop but these remained undrawn. The defendant stated that she was Russian and could not understand the order but watched what other people did.

Many similar cases were heard throughout the session. The mayor stated that unless the order was thoroughly applied, the city was in a less secure position than without it. A fortnight's grace had been given but the order had been ignored by many. It was stated that anyone breaking the order in the future could expect fines of up to £100 or six months imprisonment. In the cases before the court, most defendants were fined 10s to cover costs.

On Saturday 10 June, the ASC military sports day was held on the Recreation Ground. The local newspaper reported:

In showery weather, military sports were held in connection with the 683, 685 and 690 Companies of the M.T., A.S.C. There was a fairly good attendance on the Recreation Ground, considering the weather. The programme comprised of ten events.

The events included the 100 yards flat race, throwing a cricket ball, three-legged race, wheelbarrow race, boxing, quarter-mile flat race, sack race, officers' race, and blindfold boxing.

The prizes were presented by Mrs Campbell and there were many cheers for the officers involved in the events.

The St James's Mission Band provided the music during the afternoon.

During June, Tom Fitzgerald wrote of his company's sports events at the front. The letter was published in the *Bath Chronicle* and read:

During June, the artistes at the Palace Theatre entertained the wounded soldiers at the hospital. Lieutenant-Colonel Bannatyne, in charge of the hospital, wrote to Mr W. S. Pearce, of the Palace Theatre, saying: 'Dear Sir, Will you allow me to thank you for the splendid entertainment you provided for the wounded here on Friday and also convey my grateful thanks to all who so kindly helped? The men are most grateful for anything that takes their thoughts off their sufferings and nothing seems to help them more than such entertainments.'

And such is this war! Yesterday, a magnificent day, and under a blue sky and burning sun, we held our divisional sports, organized and run on such lines as would have done us credit had they been run at Aldershot. Yet we were within a two-hour motor car run of the firing line of the world's greatest war.

The usual military sports meeting, with all its side shows, the three balls a penny coconut shies (for which oranges were substituted), the generously-painted Aunt Sally, shies at the Kaiser and Little Willie, the racy music of the division brass band, the fancy costumes, the Early Briton, the cowboy, the two French gentlemen of the Revolution period, who caused so much amusement, the Red Indian, the typical English country wench and many others.

Oh, yes, and who was the attractive young lady who caused such a stir among the officers, and weren't some of them very disappointed when they found out who she (?) really was?

Then the officers' enclosure, with its white pipe-clayed ropes, and divisional flag flying, and the officers' refreshment tent (was there ever such luxury before?), with the real china tea cups and wonderful creations in fancy cakes. Then the other side of the tent for the more 'sporty' members, who could indulge in whiskies and soda, cigars, cigarettes etc., ad lib, all supplied gratis by the General.

The sports themselves were just great. The keenness shown by the competitors, their spirit and dash, were well worthy of the great division to which they belong. In addition, there was an exhibition of that wonderful new instrument of warfare, the ——, but enough of secrets, or the censor will intervene.

Afterwards, the prize giving, those for bayonet fighting, both for officers and men, and the mule race, all being taken by the famous 8th. The Brigade did splendidly too. Next, three cheers for the General; he seemed quite overcome by the enthusiasm – splendid fellow. Finally, of course, 'God Save the King.'

And still the battle for Verdun continues, the ceaseless swaying of the thin line from the Channel to Switzerland, the constant give and take of life. These things didn't seem to affect our sports – but before next winter? – I wonder! Mais c'est la guerre!

On Friday 16 June, a special matinee performance was given at the

The clean and tidy No 9 ward of the Bath War Hospital showing patients and staff.

Electric Theatre in Westgate Street for the wounded soldiers convalescing at the War Hospital at Combe Park. About 120 men attended together with Wardmaster Payne. The full weekend programme was watched as well as the film *Charlie at the Bank*. In the

A topical postcard featuring a Tommy at the Front showing a soldier protecting his rear end with the caption 'I ain't riskin' havin' me bloomin' brains blown out'. Even with all that went on around them, British Tommies still kept their sense of humour.

interval, soldiers were given packets of cigarettes by the manager's son and daughter, Master Eric and Miss Margery Parker. The cigarettes were a gift from the proprietor, Mr. Davis. On behalf of the men, Wardmaster Payne expressed thanks to the management for an

A busy scene at Milsom Street. During June 1916, Alexandra Day was held in the popular thoroughfare of Milsom Street. Ladies of the Red Cross sold roses and flags. The proper name of the event was Queen Alexandra's Rose Day and it was a means to raise funds for local hospitals.

enjoyable afternoon. The Bath Tramways Corporation supplied special trams to take the men to and from the theatre.

The *Bath Chronicle and Weekly Gazette* of Saturday 17 June reported on a visit to the Bath War Hospital by the artistes of the Palace Theatre. The story read:

The Englishman is noted the world over for his wonderful

adaptability. He jog-trots along, every new happening that comes up being quite an ordinary occurrence by the next day; one minute agog at some appalling news, the next rejoicing over some small feat, but always sure in his own heart of a great victory in the finish, be it two months or two years distant. He sees the splendid boys in khaki and says 'Bless 'em; they're made of fine stuff; wait until they get out there, we'll show the Germans what we can do.' Or he sees a Jack Tar and, with equal pride, says 'I don't wonder the cowards stay in Kiel Canal.' Then, alas, he sees the lighter blue with the red ties and, sighing, says 'Poor chaps, heroes every one of them, what a shame!' And so echoes everyone.

But, seeing two, or perhaps three, in the street walking casually along, does not leave anything like the same feeling in the mind as a visit to the Bath War Hospital; that new and wonderful building full of our heroes, some poor fellows still far too ill to be seen, some just able to be pushed about on long couches, some moved in a sitting position in wheel chairs and the luckier ones able to walk about, one and all so well plucked as to look with a smile on all they behold, nursed by cheerful kindly nurses headed by the most wonderful matron in the obviously loved and popular Miss Hill. Perhaps Friday last was one of the happiest days possible on which to make their acquaintance, for were not the artistes appearing at the Palace Theatre last week, by the kind permission of Mr W S Pearce, going to spend the afternoon in entertaining them?

The char-a-banc which was kindly lent by Mr Bryant, of the Bristol Company's taxi garage, free of charge, started from the Palace at about 2 o'clock, full of kind friends, one and all eager to help give a little pleasure. Management, friends, artistes and musical instruments all safely aboard, the journey was commenced and the War Hospital reached safely. A member of the RAMC signalled the char-a-banc safely through the gate and it sped on until the main building was reached where the entertainment was to be held. Then the party were conducted by nurses along what seemed numberless corridors to the large dining hall, with all the tables drawn to one end and arranged together to make a platform and a very good one too. The rest of the hall was full of chairs of all descriptions. Cigarettes, which had been brought in hundreds, were generously supplied by the staff of the Palace and their friends and these were first of all distributed. A beautiful bouquet from Mr W S Pearce was then presented to the Matron by Miss Rose Sartella, who also presented a huge armful of flowers from the same donor to 'the boys'. When she called for someone to fetch them, a wounded veteran from the front row was wheeled forward in a huge armchair to receive them amid loud cheers. He carefully nursed them all through the performance. The entertainment then began. Mr Ed Ford made a short but rousing speech and then his drolleries made the poor fellows laugh until they cried. One of the 'tit-bits' of his turn was the song 'I do like a nice cold bath.' Then followed in quick succession Mr Melidus on the xylophone and banjo; Miss Hillier with a song; the Gotham Quartette in a medley of wonderful song; the Martinis in two clever dances; and Miss Patti Clay (contralto) and Miss Williamson (soprano) with songs. Signor Cassini and Miss Sartella rendered the ever popular duet from 'Cavalerria Rusticana' in splendid voice and last came Mr Tolhurst on the piano.

The accompanists were Mr Chas H Harrison and Mr Tolhurst and the arrangements were admirably supervised by the Palace stage manager, Mr Laing and the secretary, Mr Chas. Wallace.

Alexandra Day in Bath as published in t Bath Chronicle of Saturday 1 July 1916. The photo shows a decorated car used fo the purpose of advertising Alexandra Da The group of ladies shown were involvea the effort. Mrs Donald Ackland, the own of the car, can be seen standing in the middle of the picture. Also shown is Mrs Napier (the honorary secretary) sitting ir the front seat of the car, and Mrs Victor Ames sitting on the step.

Miss Lavington's stall in Westgate Street for Alexandra Day during 1916.

Mrs Victor Ames selling to the navy and army during Alexandra Day, as published in the Bath Chronicle of Saturday 1 July 1916.

Mrs Thompson's stall at the Guildhall during Alexandra Day.

Mrs Mackintyre and Mrs Walwyn's stall in the Abbey Churchyard during Alexandra Day, as published in the Bath Chronicle of Saturday 1 July 1916.

Miss Fortune's stall in New Bond Street during Alexandra Day, as published in the Bath Chronicle of Saturday 1 July 1916.

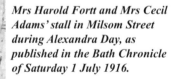

Mrs Harold Fortt and Mrs Cecil Adams' stall in Milsom Street during Alexandra Day, as published in the Bath Chronicle of Saturday 1 July 1916.

A vote of thanks to the aristes for the enjoyable concert was proposed by Mr E Tylee in the absence of Colonel Bannatyne.

As the Battle of the Somme raged in Europe, relatives back in Bath dreaded a knock on the door, as they had throughout the war, of the telegram boy bringing news of their loved ones' death. Newspapers carried the news of all wounded and killed soldiers.

The death columns of the local newspapers provided a pointer to the extent of the tragedies of Jutland and of the first Battle of the Somme. An eye-witness reported:

We passed along the line of German ships some miles away. The air was heavy with masses of smoke black, yellow, green, of every colour, which drifted between the opposing lines. Again and again salvoes of shells fell short of the mark. I watched the Iron Duke swinging through the seas, letting off broadside after broadside, wicked tongues of flames leaping through clouds of smoke. The din of battle was stunning, stupendous, deafening, as hundreds of the heaviest guns in the world gave tongue at once. All officers on board the Indefatigable, the Defence and the Black Prince were lost; only four of the Queen Mary and two of the Invincible were saved. The list of officers killed numbers 333, and included Rear Admirals Hood, and Arbuthnot, whose flags were carried on the Invincible and Defence respectively.

On 27 September, a case came before the Bath magistrates involving

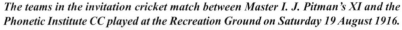

The teams in the invitation cricket match between Master I. J. Pitman's XI and the Phonetic Institute CC played at the Recreation Ground on Saturday 19 August 1916.

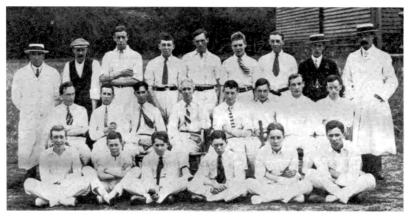

The players in the match between Bath and a team of Canadians at the Recreation Ground on Saturday 19 August 1916.

Patrick Joseph Biggs, a member of the Canadian Military Police stationed at Prior Park. The accused was charged with assaulting PC William Rogers in Wells Road on the previous Tuesday. He was further charged with assaulting Sidney Bond, at the same time and place, by violently kicking him, and also with assaulting E. Esther of the Canadian Discharge Depot, also at the same time and place.

The magistrates were Messrs E. E. Phillips (in the chair), J. Allon Tucker and F. W. Spear. The prisoner pleaded not guilty.

PC Rogers said he was called upon on Tuesday evening and on arriving at the bottom of Wells Road, he came across the prisoner, standing on the footway, having an altercation with another military man. Another man was lying in the gutter unconscious and was taken to the Royal United Hospital by ambulance. The accused than acted in a violent way, 'flashing about' and knocking down both men and women as quick as he could. Eventually, he was apprehended and taken into custody. When he was taken to the cells, he said to the policeman, 'You're an old man, old enough to be my father and I'm sorry for what I've done.'

Albert Hale, an inspector on the Bath Tramways, and Charles Cowley, a confectioner, gave further evidence that stated the trouble in Wells Road was the sequel to an incident earlier on a tram. Mr Douglas Hatt, a passenger, said he saw the accused and another soldier get off the tram. They got across the road and both fell heavily into the gutter, although not a blow was struck. Several women witnessed the event.

Sidney Bond of 10 Lyncombe Place said he noticed the soldier lying in the gutter and said he was breathing heavily. He loosened his coat and placed his cap under his head. While he was doing so, the accused assaulted him.

Lieutenant Jones of the Canadian Depot said that Biggs had never been punished for drunkenness. He further said that he had served in France and was invalided because of shell-shock and shell concussion. He said that after such an experience, a man was likely to act strangely at any time. His conduct as a soldier had been exemplary and his commanding officer had sent a man to help him.

The accused mentioned that he had been wounded in France when he took the stand under oath. He said the trouble started when he decided to eject a fellow soldier who was taking off his puttees, which he felt would annoy other passengers. He'd got to the door of the tram with the other man when, in the darkness, they both missed their footing and fell. A crowd of young hooligans came from the other side of the street and 'started to raise Cain'. They were joined by some women, who had misinterpreted the situation and became hostile because they thought he had assaulted his comrade. The accused said he had spent seven months a prisoner in Germany and admitted he had lost control of himself and couldn't remember all that had happened.

The bench decided to hand the accused over to the military authorities and requested that his commanding officer deal leniently with him. He took into account his apology to the policeman. Lieutenant Jones replied: 'I'll see that, sir.'

'It is my own conviction,' concluded the chairman, 'that he is a very good sort of fellow.'

Lieutenant Jones and Biggs thanked the bench for their decision.

At the end of September, two hospital trains arrived in the city carrying a further 120 wounded soldiers, who were returning from the Somme. More were expected later in the day. The train was expected to arrive in the afternoon but it was midnight before it reached the Midland Station. A muster of Red Cross stretcher-bearers worked to the small hours of the morning, under the supervision of Mr C. W. Adams, assisted by Quartermaster A. J. Taylor. There were eight officers and fifty-eight men on parade. The rain had recently stopped and so made the task of the police and the Somerset Volunteer Regiment somewhat easier. The Volunteer Regiment were guarding the approach to make sure they were free of any obstacles. It was reported that there was a lack of spectators, who were known to gather at the station whenever soldiers returned. Lieutenant Barkus was in command and was aided by Inspector Baker, of the police force, as well as PS Fussell. Mrs Napier and her band of female helpers worked energetically supplying refreshments to the patients. The wounded were received by Dr G. A. Bannatyne, the commandant at the Bath War Hospital, and Dr R. J. H. Scott of the Red Cross. Councillor Tom Stone paid his fifth visit to the station and handed out cigarettes to all of the men, although three turned out to be non-smokers.

There were eighteen motor ambulances in attendance and Captain H. G. Kersley of the Somerset Volunteer Regiment supervised this department of the work. Vehicles were sent by the War Hospital, the Red Cross Society and the Bath St John Ambulance Association. The 719th Company of the ASC, stationed at the Royal Victoria Park, provided ten more vehicles. Superintendent A. B. Moore of the St John Ambulance Association and his staff gave valuable assistance loading and unloading the ambulances.

The *Bath Chronicle* of Saturday 30 September reported that the request of the mayor for some relaxation of the Lighting Restriction Order had been rejected by the home secretary. The mayor had asked for the lighting order to be modified by half-an-hour in the evening to help local businesses. He was told that the lighting hours were fixed after consultation with military authorities and were necessary for safety.

The *Chronicle* reported that another claimant had arisen for the title of 'Bath's Youngest Soldier'. Trooper S. J. Keyworth of the North Somerset Yeomanry celebrated his 17th birthday in September but had been in the army for eighteen months. He enlisted in Bath when he was just 15 after giving his age as 19. In civilian life, he had been an apprentice at Messrs Stothert and Pitt's. He had been on active service for fourteen months and had experience of fighting at Ypres and other places. He'd had no leave since he'd crossed the Channel. His

Bath lady conductors and drivers. A few of the Bath lady tram conductors and drivers who operated the service while men were away fighting. Published in the Bath Chronicle and Weekly Gazette of Saturday 7 October 1916.

Mrs James, the matron, and boys of the Sutcliffe School who sold flags during Lifeboat Saturday to raise vitally needed funds. The boys are wearing caps lent by the crew of the Burnham Lifeboat. The photo appeared in the Bath Chronicle and Weekly Gazette of Saturday 7 October 1916.

stepfather, of 132 Carlton Road, was the caretaker at the Picturedrome in Southgate Street.

As reported in the *Western Daily Press* of Monday 16 October, Prior

Park in Bath had been used as a Casualty and Discharge Depot for Canadian troops since early spring. The depot was transferred to

The Bath Rugby FC played a match for war funds during October 1916, their opponents being a team representing the Army Cyclist Corps from Chiseldon, Swindon. The photo shows the two teams with the Bath team wearing striped jerseys.

Bath City FC played their first match of the season one Saturday when they entertained a team of the London Rifle Brigade, as featured in the Bath Chronicle and Weekly Gazette of Saturday 7 October 1916.

Young ladies selling flags to soldiers at the football match on the Bath City football ground during October 1916 to raise funds for the lifeboat.

The Canadians leaving Bath on Sunday 15 October 1916. Each man was presented with a Bath bun. Mr D. A. Evans (chairman of the Bath Chamber of Commerce) can be seen distributing the welcome gifts to the troops.

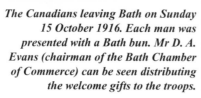

The Bath Chronicle and Weekly Gazette of Saturday 21 October 1916 carried the story of a military wedding at Christ Church. The caption read: 'The wedding took place at Christ Church, on Saturday, of Lieutenant W. Pert, of the Royal Scots Fusiliers, son of the late Mr and Mrs Pert, of Montrose, Forfar, and Miss Elsie Agnes Walker, daughter of Mr and Mrs A. Walker of 17 Northampton Street, Bath. The bridegroom has seen severe fighting and has been twice wounded.'

another part of England and on 15 October, 500 Canadians and staff left Bath on the Great Western Railway. A large number of men also left the day before.

During October, Harry Patch was conscripted as a private into the Duke of Cornwall's Light Infantry where he served as an assistant gunner. Private Patch was born at Combe Down and was the son of a stonemason. When he left school in 1913, he became an apprentice plumber in Bath. During his time in the army he was sent to Passchendaele, where he was injured by shellfire. He was returned to England on 23 December 1917, and was still convalescing when the armistice was announced in 1918.

On 28 October, the *Bath Chronicle and Gazette* announced the forthcoming visit by Miss Eva Moore. The article read:

The civic send-off to the Canadians as featured in the Bath Chronicle and Weekly Gazette of Saturday 21 October 1916. The mayor addressed a farewell message to the Canadians, who had been at Prior Park for several months. They left the city on Sunday 15 October 1916. The officer commanding the Canadians can be seen to the left of the mayor, and the town clerk of Bath (Mr F. D. Wardle) can be seen behind him.

On Monday next, at the Theatre Royal, Miss Eva Moore will pay her first visit with the delightful comedy, 'Eliza Comes to Stay,' by H. V. Esmond, which has created such an enormous success, not only in this country at the Vaudeville Theatre, but also in the United States and Canada, which Miss Moore and her husband visited not long ago. It has now played over 800 times, which speaks for itself, and as a class of play it commends itself as a comedy full of laughter all the way, which at the present time is so necessary, and anyone who enjoys a really good thoroughbred home-made farcical comedy should give 'Eliza' a hearty welcome. Eva Moore plays Eliza charmingly, delineating that subtle, yet unerring feminine instinct which says, 'I don't know why I do it but do it I must.' Her many changes of dress and doing her hair makes it an arduous part but it gives her the opportunity to show what a real artiste she is.

At the end of October, it was announced that a flying officer from Bath, Flight-Lieutenant Colin Roy Mackenzie RNAS, was to be awarded the DSO for 'his skill and gallantry in destroying a German kite balloon on September 7, 1916 under very severe anti-aircraft fire.'

The *Bath Chronicle* reported:

The feat which secured him the distinction was the destruction near Ostende of an enormous kite balloon which had been found an unmitigated nuisance. It had been flying longer than any other enemy captive balloon and, owing to the numerous German anti-aircraft guns, it was very difficult to get within striking distance of it. Travelling at a height of 13,000 feet, Lieutenant Mackenzie got well over his object and then, diving down to about 1,500 feet above the balloon, he managed to fire at it and bring it down a burning mess. His work accomplished, he had to run the gauntlet of tremendous fire from the German guns but he got away scathless, although his machine was seriously damaged.

The Bath lady tram conductors as featured in the Bath Chronicle and Weekly Gazette of Saturday 21 October 1916.

At the Holy Trinity Church, on the morning of Tuesday 7 November 1916, the wedding between Miss Daisy Louise Russell, of the Pump Room Orchestra, eldest daughter of Mr Joseph Russell, of the Pump Room Orchestra and Summer Band, and bandmaster of the 2nd Battalion Somerset Volunteer Regiment, and Mr Walter Lear, late principal clarinet, Bournemouth, and Bath Pump Room Orchestra, and now of the DCLI, son of Mr Hiram Lear, of Newcastle-on-Tyne. A large congregation wished them well.

At St Stephen's, Lansdown, on the afternoon of Tuesday 7 November 1916, the marriage of Leonard Robert Warner Allen Shuter, Kent Fortress Royal Engineers, son of Mr and Mrs Allen Shuter, of Horton, Kirby, Kent, and Alice Margaret Alexandra, daughter of Mr and Mrs Foote, of Newland House, Lansdown, Bath, was solemnised very quietly. The Bath Chronicle and Weekly Gazette of Saturday 11 November 1916.

A photo of three Bathonians taken while they were recuperating in a hospital in Valetta, Malta, during November 1916. They were – Back row: Mr S. Latcham (ASC) and Mr A. Stone (ASC), son of Councillor Tom Stone. Sitting in the bath chair is Mr Meddick (RFA).

Private W. Hussey, formerly a Bath corporation employee who was awarded the Military Medal, as reported on Saturday November 1916.

In November, the newspapers reported the attempted suicide, at home, of Private Brackstone of the 4th Company, Cambridge Regiment. He was found by his wife, Mrs A. H. Brackstone, and was bleeding profusely from a wound in his throat, which was self-inflicted. A pair of scissors used for the purpose were laying nearby. She telephoned the police at 2.50 am and Inspector Baker sent PS Maynard and PC Brown to the house. The officers decided that the case was one for medical treatment and called the Bath Fire Brigade motor ambulance at 3.10 am. The patient was driven to the Royal United Hospital and was attended to by Dr W. J. Bacque, who recommended that he be transferred to the Bath War Hospital at Combe Park.

Private and Mrs Brackstone had been married two years. On Friday 24 November, Private Brackstone was collected from the hospital by his father, who had travelled from Doncaster. It was stated that his health had been indifferent for some time.

Captain E. B. Hope, who was reported as wounded in action in the newspaper of Saturday 4 November 1916.

THIS TABLET WAS ERECTED TO COMMEMORATE THE FACT THAT DURING HIS MAYORALTY ALDERMAN HARRY THOMAS HATT J.P. WAS TWICE CALLED UPON TO BEAR THE GRIEVOUS LOSS OF A SON EACH OF WHOM LAID DOWN HIS LIFE FOR HIS COUNTRY ON THE FIELD OF BATTLE IN FRANCE.

CAPT ARTHUR BEECH HATT (SOMERSET LIGHT INFANTRY) FELL ON THE 1ST DAY OF JULY 1916.

CAPT EDWARD BEECH HATT (SOMERSET LIGHT INFANTRY) FELL ON THE 8TH DAY OF AUGUST 1916.

THE MEMBERS OF THE BATH CITY COUNCIL DESIRE TO RECORD IN THIS LASTING FORM THE HEROISM OF THE SONS AND THE SACRIFICE OF THE PARENTS.

The memorial to the ex-mayor's officer sons. The memorial tablet in Bath Guildhall to Captains A. B. Hatt and E. B. Hatt, the two sons of the ex-mayor of Bath, both of whom were killed in action. The tablet was unveiled on Thursday 9 November 1916. The Bath Chronicle and Weekly Gazette of Saturday 11 November 1916.

'Bath's Australian Guests', as pictured in the Bath Chronicle of Saturday 18 November 1916. Many soldiers from Australia were stationed in the city during the war before leaving to fight at the Front.

A photo of a group of Australian soldiers stationed in Bath as featured in the Bath Chronicle of Saturday 18 November 1916.

In December, a Christmas message from the mayoress to Bath's women workers appeared in the *Chronicle*. It read:

I think that there are few who will maintain that women's position in England, at the end of the present year, is the same as it has been in the days gone by.

This war, which has awakened reverence for the heroism of men, has also taught us respect for the efficiency of women. The nation, which has called to the women bravely to give up her sons, has now called for the time, the strength and the skill of her daughters – and it is being given to the full.

A group of women doing the work of men who have left to fight in the war. Seen here at Messrs Stothert and Pitts, Bath, during November 1916.

It is not the least of my privileges during this year of office to get an insight into the magnificent work which is being done by the women of Bath. I have already come in touch with numerous organisations and the quiet self-sacrifice and steady devotion of the workers has indeed been a revelation to me.

But the times call for other things beside service. May I plead for the 'Larger Mind,' for breadth of outlook and for the magnificent temper to help us in still more difficult tasks ahead of us?

Service is measured by the inner soul and not always by the thing achieved and we need the 'deeper vision' to understand that the more awful the sacrifice which is demanded, the more worth while it is to make it.

My sincere wish for all is that this may be a Happy Christmas. Few of us in the Homeland will find it possible to keep up old customs at the Christmas season but many, I'm assured, will heartily enter into the task of preparing brightness for the lives of others and may those of us who have the added strain of public duties never forget that, first and foremost, it is the duty of the women of England 'to keep the home fires burning.'

Selina Long. The Guildhall, Bath.

December 22, 1916.

An advert for the Palace Theatre in December 1916 announcing the forthcoming appearance of Queen Leighton, who was a British music hall star. Also on the bill were Arthur Wilbey 'Versatile Comedian Warwick 'Speciality Artist', Phyl and Madge 'Song and Dances', Keen and Waller 'Celebrated Come Artistes', and the Palace Bioscope.

An advert for Revell and Sons, Military Bootmakers, which appeared in the Bath Chronicle in December 1916. The range included field boots, marching boots and rubber boots, ideal for camp- and trench-wear.

A Weston Yeoman's Wedding featured in the Bath Chronicle of Saturday 30 December 1916. The caption read: 'A wedding of considerable local interest took place at All Saints' Parish Church, Upper Weston, on Saturday afternoon, the Reverend F. A. Bromley, vicar, officiating. The bride was Katie Louise, eldest daughter of Mr Henry Stevens, and the bridegroom, Farrier-Major Alexander Felix Holcombe, North Somerset Yeomanry, second son of Mr Charles Holcombe.'

A BATH PATRIOTIC FAMILY.

MR. AND MRS. ALFRED HILL, OF ODD DOWN, BATH, HAVE SEVEN SONS SERVING IN THE ARMY, WHOSE PHOTOS WE HERE REPRODUCE:—

Private A. HILL,   Sapper CHARLES HILL,   Sapper WILLIAM HILL,

with the R.E.   with the Wessex R.E.   with the Wessex R.E.

Private FRANK HILL,   Lance-Corpl. WALTER HILL,   Private A. HILL,   Sapper GEORGE HILL,

with the Somerset L.I.   with the Canadian Highlanders.   with the Somerset L.I.   with the Wessex R.E.

A Bath patriotic family, as published in the Bath Chronicle of Saturday 30 December 1916. Mr and Mrs Alfred Hill of Odd Down, Bath, had seven sons serving in the army whose photos appeared in the newspaper. These included Private A. Hill (RE), Sapper Charles Hill (Wessex RE), Sapper William Hill (Wessex RE), Private Frank Hill (Somerset Light Infantry), Lance-Corporal Walter Hill (Canadian Highlanders), Private A. Hill (Somerset Light Infantry), and Sapper George Hill (Wessex RE).

Robert E. Vaughan, late of the 18th County of the London Regiment (London Irish Rifles), only son of Mr and Mrs A. E. Vaughan of Torbay House, Bath, was reported killed in action in newspapers during December 1916.

CHAPTER FOUR

1917 – Seeing it Through

The *Bath Chronicle* of Saturday 13 January reported on the final nights of the Christmas pantomime. The article read:

It will be with sincere regret that Theatre Royal patrons will see the curtain rung down for the last time on 'Sinbad the Sailor,' for the Bath pantomime has become an established family institution and the present season, from a popular point of view, has proved no less successful than last year's excellent production.

The marriage of Major James Yescombe Baldwin, Army Cyclist Corps, son of Lieutenant and Mrs James Baldwin, of 21 Green Park, Bath, and Ethel Gladys, eldest daughter of Mr and Mrs T. H. Miller, St Albans, Weston Park, Bath took place at St Paul's Church on Wednesday 10 January 1917. The photograph was taken on the steps of the Grand Pump Room Hotel, where the reception took place.

While the vast numbers of men who witnessed 'Aladdin' last year have necessarily been conspicuous by their absence, the feminine portion of the audience has supported 'Sinbad' most regularly and enthusiastically and many thousands of children have gladdened the hearts of their elders with their shouts of merriment and their hearty attempts to sing the chorus songs which they seem to pick up with marvellous celerity.

But Sinbad sails away for the last time next Saturday and the last week will see three particularly attractive evenings for the management have arranged a benefit night to Miss Pru Purl on Tuesday, when a host of extra attractions will be put into the programme for what is to be known as 'Sinbad's own evening.' Miss Purl should receive a very hearty welcome on Tuesday, for her work has contributed a long way to the success of the pantomime and her smartness and unflagging good humour have made her most popular with every part of the house. Few principal boys have a prettier way with children than Miss Purl and her winsome tenderness with the little mites who join her in the song 'You're my precious little baby' is one of the gems of the performance.

Among the special items for this festive Tuesday evening will be a comic interlude called 'Kier's Komedy Kultur Koros,' which will set the whole house in a roar, so intensely witty it is and full of rollicking fun. Then here and there throughout the pantomime, little surprises will be made, which will make a joyous performance on 'Sinbad's own evening.

In January, the *Bath Chronicle* told the story of a deceased soldier's

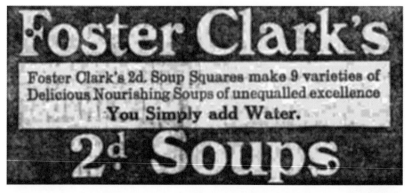

An advert for Foster Clark's Soups published on Saturday 6 January 1917. Their 2d soup squares made nine varieties of 'delicious nourishing soups of unequalled excellence.'

The Bath Chronicle and Weekly Gazette of Saturday 13 January 1917 told the story of a soldier from Bath, Sergeant Fred W. Holley, who was killed in action, and whose signet ring was returned to his fiancée, Mabel Hole.

signet ring being returned to his fiancé, Miss Mabel Alice Hole. The soldier was Sergeant Fred W. Holley, who was formerly a carter who resided at 26 Excelsior Street, Bath. He volunteered for active service at the beginning of the war after serving three years in the Grenadier Guards. He took part in the heavy fighting at the beginning of hostilities and took part in the famous retreat from France. He was twice wounded, the first wound being through his shoulder. When he recovered and returned to active service he sustained another wound to the scalp which didn't, however, require hospital treatment. He had many narrow escapes and on several occasions was completely buried in a trench. Prior to his death, he was working in the medical department with the regimental doctor and was wearing the badge of a stretcher-bearer. He had thirty men under him and was in charge of sixteen stretchers. As the battalion was fighting towards Morval, he was shot through the head and died instantaneously. His body was discovered by a Sherwood Forester who could find no means of identification on him other than a gold signet ring, which he removed. The ring bore the monogram 'F.H.' and inside was engraved 'From M.H.'. Subsequently, the Sherwood Forester was wounded and returned to England. An appeal for information as to the owner of the ring was heard by Miss Mabel Hole of Rosemount Farm, Lyncombe Vale, and she was placed in communication with the finder of the ring. By that time, he had returned to France but Miss Hole's letter reached him there and the ring was returned to her by registered post.

The *Bath Chronicle* continued the story:

In conversation with our representative, Miss Mabel A. Hole said she had kept company with Sergeant Holley for about five years and they had been engaged for two years. But for the war, they would have been married. She gave the gold ring to her fiancé twelve months last December when he was home on leave. Asked how she received the intimation that the ring had been found on the battlefield, Miss Hole said the announcement in 'John Bull' was seen by a friend in London and sent on to her. She was then informed on writing to 'John Bull' that the finder of the ring was Sergeant H.V. Barnes, of the Sherwood Foresters, and that he was at Canterbury. She wrote to him there but Sergeant Barnes had left for the front. Mrs Barnes, however, forwarded the letter, with which was a photograph of Sergeant Holley, to her husband who at once returned the ring to Miss Hole. Miss Hole said she understood that Sergeant Holley was lying for ten days on the battlefield before his body was found. She regards it as a remarkable series of events which brought back the ring into her possession and says she shall ever treasure it. Sergeant Barnes had previously received an application for the ring but did not regard it as genuine so did not part with it.

Later in January, the Bath Secondary School Old Students' Association held a concert for wounded soldiers in the city. The event took place at the Technical School and the number of soldiers who attended amounted to seventy. There was also a good attendance of old students. The soldiers were conveyed to the venue in cars lent by Captain H.G. Kersley and the programme was arranged by Mr A. Godfrey Day, the director of studies.

On Monday 5 February, the mayor held a public meeting at Bath

Families turned out to skate on the frozen canal during February 1917. The fun, due to the cold weather conditions, brought some light relief from the daily war news.

A wounded Tommy enjoys a backward slide on the ice of the frozen canal as featured in the Bath Chronicle and Weekly Gazette of Saturday 3 February 1917.

A lady skater on the frozen canal. The Bath Chronicle and Weekly Gazette of Saturday 3 February 1917 carried this photo with the caption 'A clever lady skater'.

Hard work for 'Bully' on the frozen Bath Canal. A dog is shown trying to walk on the canal accompanied by its owner dressed warmly for the cold weather in a fur coat during February 1917.

Guildhall to discuss the government appeal for patriotic citizens to support the War Loan.

The *Bath Chronicle* reported:

> *The Mayor said that it did not seem to be generally realised that we had reached a very critical state in the war. The Government had asked for men and munitions and they had got them; now they were asking for money. There was no sacrifice about it – (hear, hear) – it was simply lending. If men could lay down their lives for us we must not be backward in making what was really not a sacrifice but a simple lending of all the money we possessed to the Government, so that the war might be brought to a successful conclusion. We must trust our leaders, and our leaders had plainly told us we must place what we possess at the disposal of the Government. Now there had to be brought into existence the machinery for bringing home to every citizen of Bath the fact that he was wanted to do something. People might say they could scarcely find enough to live, and he knew that was true in a good number of cases; but the source they wanted to tap was the big wage earners and if the need were only brought home to them, they would respond as the monied people had done. People needed to spend less, to have fewer people waiting upon them and to eat less in order to meet the latest menace of the Germans that was going to affect this country very severely.*

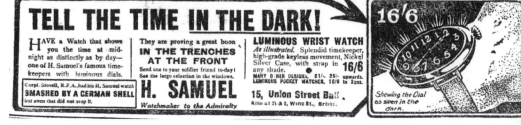

Tell the time in the dark. An advert for luminous watches, which appeared in the local newspaper of Saturday 6 January 1917. The advert stated that they were proving popular in the trenches at the Front and compelled their readers to send their soldier friends one. They were priced at 16/6. The advert announced that 'Corporal Stovell, R.F.A., had his H. Samuel watch smashed by a German shell but even that did not stop it'.

On 3 March, reports were carried in local newspapers of a crashed aeroplane. The story read:

> *Owing presumably to engine trouble, an aeroplane alighted at about 11.30 on Monday morning in a field at Kelston. The machine ran for some distance up the field before coming to a standstill and its appearance occasioned considerable panic among the cattle which were grazing there. Apparently, the aeroplane fouled a clump of trees before landing, for the pilot was forced to remain in the field for some hours.*

On 10 March, it was announced that a Combe Down footballer had been killed.

The story read:

> *Mrs Brinksworth, of 53 Entry Hill, has been informed of the death, at a Theatre of War in the Near East, of her son, Charles Brinksworth, of the Royal Field Artillery. Deceased, who was about 25 years of age, worked at the Fullers' Earth Works before joining the Army. Like several of his brothers, deceased played rugby football for Combe Down Club, his position being full back. His brothers, Arthur, Frank, Sidney, Stanley and Cecil are all in the Army and abroad. Deceased was a single man.*

On 24 March, the *Yellowstone News* in Montana carried the headline 'U.S. expected to announce that state of war exists'. The newspaper went on to report that 'News received from Plymouth that fifteen men, some of them Americans, had been drowned when the American merchantmen *Vigilancia* was sunk without warning by a German submarine'. The story also stated that 'President Wilson is expected, within 48 hours, to indicate definitely that he believes a virtual state of war exists between the United States and Germany.'

The wounded at Bath War Hospital shown during April 1917. Many have recovered well but others are seen in wheelchairs or in their beds.

On 5 April, the *Evening Herald* reported:

> *The U.S. Senate has passed the resolution declaring a state of war with Germany by 82 votes to 6 at 11.15pm after 13 hours continuous debate. There was no demonstration when the result was announced.*

America joined the war on 6 April 1917.

On Saturday 14 April, the *Bath Chronicle* carried a story under the headline 'A Boy Hero'. It read:

> *With military honours there was buried at Locksbrook Cemetery, on Thursday afternoon, Private Ernest Patterson, of the 2nd Royal Irish Regiment. Since December last, the brave lad had been an inmate of the Bath War Hospital and there he passed away, the cause of death being consumption, brought on by the rigours of the campaign abroad. He enlisted when only fifteen and had served over two years in the Army, dying at the age of seventeen. His mother was among the mourners who came to Bath for the burial in the specially reserved space for the soldiers from the War Hospital. The Reverend F A Bromley, Vicar of Weston and Chaplain of the Hospital, conducted the rites of the Church. The military guard was furnished from the RSPD, ASC and was commanded by Lieutenant Cooper, while Sergeant Price was in charge of the firing party which discharged the volleys over the soldier lad's grave. There were many comrade patients from the War Hospital at the cemetery.*

A female farm worker. Miss D. Smart, third daughter of Mr and Mrs W. F. Smart, of Little Solsbury, Batheaston, helping to do work of national importance on a nearby farm during April 1917.

Three well-known figures in Bath including Lieutenant Allen Smith (Australia), Captain Guy Little (England) and Captain A. G. Bernier (Canada), photographed in April 1917.

On the afternoon of Wednesday 2 May, a meeting took place at the Guildhall to discuss the organisation of Bath's Egg Day on 19 May. Mrs P. K. Stothert presided over a group of ladies who were aiding the event. Mrs Stothert explained that when the War Hospital was first opened, she was asked to collect eggs for it. She had been looking after a district for the National Egg Collection for the Wounded and wrote to inquire if instead of sending eggs to London she could collect for the Bath War Hospital and send the surplus to London. The people of London were very helpful providing boxes, literature, posters and receipt books so that in Bath there would be no expense at all.

Many of the eggs sent to London were then forwarded to base hospitals at the Front. Mrs Stothert reminded her helpers that the French wanted all eggs collected in France to go to their own so everything needed for British soldiers fighting abroad would have to come from England.

Mrs Stothert and her committee were thanked by Mr Egbert Lewis, the chairman of the War Hospital Committee, for their help so far, which amounted to about 1,000 eggs a week being collected.

The New Marquee Section at Bath War Hospital. Tents were erected to house the many wounded troops that needed to be cared for.

A convoy of sick and wounded men arrived at Bath Midland Station on Tuesday 29 May shortly after 3.30 pm. There were 235 cases, of which ninety were medical and 145 surgical. There was an abundance of ambulances to meet them and Captain Kersley SVR was in charge of the transport arrangements.

The patients were said to have a very war-worn appearance and looked like they had gone through a terrible ordeal. Some of the injured men hobbled painfully along the station platform to the awaiting cars at the station entrance. However, they were in excellent spirits and cheered on their comrades as they made it to the waiting vehicles. The men came from various British units as well as quite a number of Australian troops.

On 2 June, *the Bath Chronicle* reported the death of a man who had been called in for re-examination. The story read:

> *A verdict of 'Death from natural causes' was returned at an inquest on the body of Sidney Earnest Nobbs, a bootmaker, who fell dead on his way home after being medically re-examined. It was stated that he had been discharged from the Army in April 1916, suffering from heart disease, and was called up under the recent Act.*

His mother said that the authorities well knew her son's condition of health and ought not to have called him up.

The medical evidence was that the man suffered from a very severe form of heart disease.

The Coroner said that there was sedentary work now that many men who had been discharged from the Army could do. Hence the Act calling them for re-examination.

A group of happy Tommies at the Bath War Hospital, as featured in the Bath Chronicle of Saturday 30 June 1917.

A wounded soldier at Bath War Hospital. The photo appeared in the local paper of Saturday 30 June 1917 and was captioned 'How the badly wounded get about'.

The state of Bath's roads were discussed at a meeting of the Bath Surveying Committee during June. It was stated that miles of road were now in a dangerous condition and many complaints had been received. Mr Stone stated: 'We have not the requisite repair materials available and neither do the Tramways Company.' The chairman replied: 'They must fill the roads up with something.' Mr Sealy continued, 'The rate they are going on, they won't be finished in five years. We had a convoy of wounded yesterday – 200 odd men, and to take them down Upper Bristol Road was wicked. There ought to be some representation from the committee to the Tramways Company to do that piece of road at once.'

During July 1917, the trustees of Prior Park College put in a claim for compensation to the War Office over the use of the premises by the military authorities. The claim was rejected by the commission.

During July, Messrs Harbutt of the Plasticine Works at Bathampton received a letter from London. It read:

You will be interested to know that we have just had a call from a lieutenant serving with the Tyneside Scottish. The lieutenant, on returning to the front in February, took with him a large supply of Plasticine and he tells us with this material he modelled about 2,000 yards of the Arras front. This model was extremely useful in preparing the officers for the important advance that was made there a short time ago. So successful indeed was the result of the lieutenant's model that he expects to be fully engaged on this sort of work in future. His method of procedure is rather interesting. He first works out the contours in Plasticine, packing up the higher elevations with paper or papier-mâché. The trenches, enemy trenches, ruined houses, trees used for range finding and other items are then shown in different colours. The names of the various houses, villages, farms etc., are printed on small slips of paper and attached to the model. Unfortunately, the lieutenant tells us that the Arras model was lost when they moved from that neighbourhood after the advance, or we should have an opportunity of seeing this specimen of his work which played so important a part in the general plan.

The wounded soldiers, nurses and staff of W.3 tents at the Bath War Hospital during July 1917. Some wounded soldiers can be seen in their beds in the picture.

In July, Gertrude Hill of 26 Hampton View was summoned to court for an offence against the Lighting Restriction Order. It was stated that at 12.55 am on 12 July, a constable had seen a light burning in the house. The defendant stated that her husband was away fighting in France and she only lit the gas to show some friends his photograph. She pleaded guilty and was fined 5 shillings.

King Edward School OTC Inspection on the recreation ground during July 1917. The headmaster of the school stated that the number of Old Edwardians serving in the Officer Training Corps was 460.

The OTC Inspection on the recreation ground during July 1917. The headmaster of King Edward School was asked if he knew if there were many boys of age and physical ability at the school who did not belong to the OTC. He replied: 'Very few, and then there are special reasons. I think the whole of the sixth form of more than 20 boys, except one, are in the corps.'

On Wednesday 18 July, two deserters appeared before magistrates. Archibald Coats, aged 25, was charged with being a deserter from the Royal Naval Reserve since November 1915. William Gardiner, aged 32, was also charged with being a deserter from the ASC. Both men pleaded guilty. PC Burbidge had arrested the men in Locksbrook Road on Tuesday afternoon. When he noticed they were wearing army shirts, he stopped to question them. They told him that they had been on the 'tramp' and had come from Gloucester. Gardiner told a witness that he had deserted six months previously. Both men were remanded until an escort could meet them. The police constable was rewarded five shillings in each case.

In the personal column of the *Bath Chronicle* of Saturday 11 August appeared the notice:

Girl, fond of fairy tales, cathedrals, warm colour and the south, travelling, tramping, laughter and fun, books, pictures, old gardens and music would like to hear from anyone of similar tastes. Please write characteristically to F38, Bath office of this paper.

The picture featured in the Bath Chronicle of Saturday 28 July 1917 under the heading 'Bath boys in India'. Shown in the photo are: Back, Private Frank Payne (Somersets), son of Mr W. T. Payne, Widcombe Hill. Left, Lance-Corporal A. E. Manns (Somersets) of 15 Pulteney Grove. Right, Private Stanley Loader (Somersets) of Ontago House, Larkhall. Front, Private A. V. Glisson (Devons) of 16 Pulteney Grove.

With many men away fighting and unable to supervise their children, lots of boys appeared in court. In the *Bath Chronicle* of Saturday 11 August, a selection of current cases appeared:

> *Frederick Little, aged 12, of Cheltenham Street was charged on remand in the Juvenile Court with stealing a 10 shilling treasury note belonging to his sister. The boy pleaded guilty and arrangements were made to send him to the Nautical School at Portishead until he was 16. His parents agreed to contribute 2 shillings a week towards his maintenance.*
>
> *William Reardon, aged 17, appeared in court for using bad language. He denied the charge. P.C. Lane said that he was in the Gravel Walk, near Brock Street, at 1.30am when he heard talking. He discovered the defendant and five others sitting smoking and discussing house breaking. Reardon, using bad language, asked the group who among them was game for a bit of house-breaking or stealing apples. The bad language could be heard in Brock Street and when P.C. Lane appeared, the boys scattered although he was able to apprehend Reardon. Reardon resisted arrest and once at the station, refused to give the names of the other boys. The bench imposed a fine of £1 or 14 days and allowed the youth time to pay.*

On Saturday 15 September, the *Bath Chronicle* reported on the absence of black horses at funeral services.

The article read:

> *At several funerals which have taken place recently in the city, brown horses have been employed to draw the hearse and mourning coaches. This, I understand, is not the result of a war shortage of black horses but the outcome of a direct request that the traditional sombre associations of funerals should be, to some extent, abandoned. This is a hopeful sign, particularly in times of all-prevailing sadness such as these. No good purpose can be gained by over-emphasis of the gloomy associations of death. We have already liberated ourselves largely from the depressing surroundings of the funerals described in the pages of Dickens. The further we can progress in that direction the better.*

The *Bath Chronicle*, also on Saturday 15 September, carried a story under the headline 'A Soldier's Worries'. It read:

Thomas William White, a private in the A.S.C. and formerly a clerk, was brought up on remand charged with attempting suicide on August 23rd by cutting his left wrist with a razor at his quarters.

The magistrates were the Mayor (in the chair), Alderman E.E. Phillips, Alderman J. Rubie and Mr. H.G. Kersley.

Lieutenant William Cook, R.A.M.C., said that the prisoner was brought to the War Hospital early in the morning with wounds that were not dangerous to life. Across the front of the left wrist was a wound, approximately 3 inches, but no important vessels were divided. On the front of the right wrist was a wound two inches long and here one artery was involved.

By the Clerk: White did not become unconscious from hemorrhage; he was sure of that.

The Clerk: You do not think that if he had been left alone after making these cuts that he would have died? – No, certainly not.

Witness added that the man gave no trouble in the hospital and two days before he was discharged, he told the witness that he was very sorry it happened. He didn't know what made him do it but he had had a lot of trouble at home for two years and it had worried him greatly. The night before that had occurred, he slept at the top of the building and, on account of an old-standing trouble, it was necessary for him to get up at night. In going down a strange staircase in the dark, he missed his footing and fell. Next morning he felt that the whole world was against him. Witness considered that as he had had worry at home for a prolonged period – two years – with his health being only fair, and being suddenly plunged into new and strange surroundings, it rather upset his balance for the time being. Witness considered he would be all right in the service if he gave himself time to settle down to the new conditions.

A lieutenant in the A.S.C. said that he understood from the adjutant that everything would be done to make White as comfortable as possible.

The Mayor, in telling prisoner that they would hand him over to the military authorities, said that he must not think that he was going to get out of his troubles by doing a foolish thing like that. The best thing in entering into new conditions was to face them manfully and make up his mind he would do what was asked of him. Would he give an undertaking that so far as he could he would make himself an efficient soldier? – Prisoner said he would and desired to thank the doctor for what he had said on his behalf.

He was then handed over to the military authority.

Boys of St Mark's School at the Cross Bath. The photo appeared in the Bath Chronicle of Saturday 22 September 1917.

The pupils of Weymouth House Girls' School. The photo appeared under the headline 'Bath schoolgirls whose relatives were fighting the country's battles' on Saturday 22 September 1917.

The girls attending Weymouth House Girls' School. The Bath Chronicle reported: 'All these children have either a father or a brother in the Army; in fact there is only one girl in the school who has not a relative serving.'

On Saturday 20 October, the *Bath Chronicle* carried a story about a Bath man who now walked with the aid of artificial legs. The story read:

> *Numerous accounts have been forthcoming of the wonderful way in which maimed soldiers are turned out of the special hospital at Roehampton with missing limbs replaced so cleverly that it is sometimes difficult for anyone seeing these restored soldiers to tell which of their limbs have been supplied by nature and which has been forthcoming from the art of man. So remarkably successful are these artificial appliances that it is stated that the brave fellows who have had them fitted are very little handicapped in getting about and some, in fact, can not merely walk with ease but actually run and jump.*
>
> *On some of the many occasions on which Mr. W.S. Pearce has kindly arranged matinees at the Palace Theatre for wounded soldiers, it was noticed that a soldier maimed to the extent of having lost the lower part of both legs was wheeled in to witness the entertainments. He was then virtually helpless. Since then he has been to Roehampton and is now independent of wheelchairs in as much that he can get about perfectly easy on his artificial feet and*

The Somerset Regiment. The 2nd Battalion of Prince Albert's (Somerset) Light Infantry. The unit remained in Quetta, India throughout the war.

legs. He has had the appliances only a month and has, naturally, not got thoroughly used to them but the facility with which he walks is the amazement of himself and his friends alike.

The soldier who has thus been transformed from helplessness to activity is a Bath man, ex-Private George Harold Edwards, Gloucester Regiment, whose experiences as a member of the original B.E.F., which crossed to the continent in August 1914, would, if fully recorded, fill a book.

Private Edwards had been injured at Ypres and Loos before recovering and being sent back into battle. While fighting at the Somme in July 1916, he was hit by a German percussion bomb, which shattered both of his legs.

On Friday 9 November, Dr Preston King was elected the new mayor of Bath. He had held the position in 1914 when war broke out. The retiring mayor (Mr C. H. Long) was commended by Councillor F. W. Spear and Major-General Bradshaw. Thanking the council for his election, Dr Preston King expressed the hope that rationing of food and fuel would shortly be introduced in order that all, rich and poor, might be on an equal footing.

On Thursday 15 November, Eleanor Buckbeims, of 4 Gay Street, appeared at the Bath police court charged with failing to report her change of address in accordance with the Aliens Restriction Order. Detective Inspector Burge said that he saw the defendant in Gay Street and she gave her nationality as British but said that her husband was German. She explained that she had not lived with him for seven years and didn't ever intend to do so again. She told the detective that she hadn't registered and would rather die than sign her name as a German. She explained that she had applied to the Home Office to re-register as British. The bench stated that by this admission, she must have realised that she was currently registered as German. She was fined 10 shillings to cover court costs.

On 1 December, a meeting of the Bath Board of Guardians was convened, presided by Colonel E. P. Clayton, to discuss Christmas arrangements for the poor old people in their care. It was announced that the 'extras' this year would cost £7 3s less than last year. The additional items for Christmas had cost £25 the previous year and part of the saving had been due to this year's plum pudding. It was stated that samples of the proposed pudding had been tasted by the committee and were said to be 'very good'. The ingredients to be used were raisins, treacle, carrots, suet, maize flour, milk and spice. Regular ingredients such as wheat flour, sugar, currants, peel and eggs were excluded.

Offers of gifts of beer and mineral water came from Messrs Biggs, Coventry, Fuller, Southwood, Stride and H. Williams, which were gratefully accepted.

Mr Southwood, of the Guardians, stated: 'The poor old people need that gift more than ever. Those giving the beer and mineral water could ill afford to do it but they were going to do it if they went without themselves.' This was met with laughter from the board. He continued: 'The poor people have been cut down in everything.'

When he visited the house the previous week, he said that the inmates had asked him if they were going to have their glass of beer this year. He continued that they had sons and grandsons away fighting in the war and when the latter learned that their relatives were having one day made lighter and happier, that they would commend the Board of Guardians. This was seconded by Mr Cox. A vote was taken and, although there were two dissentients, it was decided to let the elderly have their beer.

It was agreed at the meeting that women and children who are in receipt of out-relief should be allowed an extra shilling for Christmas.

On Saturday 22 December, the Palace Theatre announced that this year's pantomime, *Cinderella*, would be opening the following week,

Members of the Women's Army Auxiliary Corps who arrived in Bath in December 1917.

An advert for Cinderella, the Christmas pantomime of 1917. The show broke the box office records of the previous seven years.

opening on Christmas Eve. Due to the length of the show, the curtains rose at 7.15 pm continuing until 10.20 pm.

Over at the Palace was *The Kirchner Girl*, described as 'a superb living reproduction of Raphael Kirchener's World-renowned Pictures'. The footnote mentioned: 'These true art pictures are reproduced in exact detail and by specially-selected models. The art world has pronounced them as the most perfect colouring and most gorgeous type of female beauty.' Also on the bill was 'Tambo and Tambo' featuring 'their dazzling manipulation of tambourines'.

The War Bond Coach. The stagecoach that started from the Guildhall and toured the principal thoroughfares of the city for about an hour starting at 3 pm during December 1917. Just as it was being driven from the Guildhall, the first war bond was sold, which was paid for with gold. In the coach, ten to a dozen wounded soldiers were sat and the sides carried banners reading 'Rally around the boys and buy War Bonds', 'Attack the enemy with your money – buy War Bonds', and 'Buy War Bonds at 20 High Street.'

The Argyle Girl Guides gave two performances of The Babes in the Woods with the purpose of clearing the £4 deficit in their funds and also raising money for the Bath War Hospital. The performance was arranged by Private Robert Percival ASC and Mrs Percival, assisted by Miss Clifford (captain of the Guides) and Mr and Mrs E. H. Horstmann.

On Christmas Eve, carols were sung at the Bath War Hospital. One party was made up of nursing staff and wounded men singing around the tents and another was made up of ladies and gentlemen from outside the hospital who sang whilst walking through all the wards. The singing went on from eight to nine o'clock. The festivities carried on in the wards which were decorated by the men with evergreens and mottoes. The Red Cross had collected together enough money to give each man in the hospital a gift. This consisted of a little wallet or pocketbook with the words 'Bath War Hospital' stamped on it. In addition, crackers and apples had been sent from the Red Cross depot and the profits of the Bath Bun (the hospital publication) were also put to good use. The Canadian Red Cross Society had sent £16 so that all the Canadians in the hospital could have a gift of some socks. The Australians also received gifts of wallets from London. Every patient had a meal of turkey and plum pudding. This required the Red Cross to supply forty-eight turkeys for the purpose. Entertainment also included music, whist drives and competitions.

From two to four o'clock, visitors were admitted, although because tramcars weren't running, not many turned up. Nearly every ward had its own piano and there was always one of the wounded men ready to entertain his comrades. Miss Hill, the matron, was helped by her loyal staff and the kitchen staff, under Mrs Mallett and Miss Meade made approximately 1,200 sausage rolls, cooked forty-eight turkeys and also made a large number of plum puddings. The men greatly appreciated everything and the celebration was described as 'top-hole'.

At the Red Cross Auxiliary at Bathampton House, Christmas dinner included an abundance of turkey, plum pudding, crystallised fruit and ginger beer. All were said to have 'rare fun' with the contents of the crackers. At 3 pm, the men gathered around a 10ft wonderfully illuminated tree, donated by Mr Mallett, and received gifts. Staff of the hospital were also given presents. The matron received a pair of topaz earrings. The quartermaster received a luminous watch in a handsome case, and the commandant received from the staff a beautiful leather-bound blotter, bearing her initials, a fountain pen and other gifts. Lady de Blaquiere, in the name of the patients, gave a hearty vote of thanks to the commandant, the matron and staff for giving everyone such a wonderful Christmastide. She said that she hoped that there wouldn't be too many more Christmases spent at war.

Bath's War Bond Effort, as published in the Bath Chronicle and Weekly Gazette of Saturday 29 December 1917. The poster reads: 'Help to build Bath's War Bond Tank. Put in your bit here. Every square represents £100.' A man on a ladder can be seen adding a piece to the picture of the displayed tank.

The pristine kitchen at the Bath War Hospital. The staff were kept continuously busy supplying meals to the many wounded servicemen who were recuperating at the hospital.

CHAPTER FIVE

1918 – The Final Blows

In January 1918, sugar was rationed. By the end of April, meat, butter, margarine and cheese were also rationed. Ration cards were issued and people were required to register with their local butcher and grocer. People in Bath joined long queues to get the most basic of foods, including potatoes and many other vegetables.

Spring Gardens Road and the Recreation Ground under water after heavy flooding during January 1918.

An announcement in the local newspaper on 12 January read:

The Morning Post on Monday stated that the second contingent of released British prisoners of war which arrived at Scheveningen,

Holland, on Saturday night, consisting of 43 officers and 248 non-commissioned officers and men, is in charge of Colonel Bond, of the King's Own Yorkshire Light Infantry. This is Lieutenant-Colonel R.C. Bond, D.S.O., a brother of Mrs. Preston King, Mayoress of Bath, who is naturally delighted to hear the good news that her brother is at last out of the hands of the Huns. Colonel Bond was taken prisoner while commanding a battalion of the Yorkshires at Mons. Another of the Mayoress's brothers is Major-General F.G. Bond, C.B., who has done excellent work at the War Office as an Assistant Director. His son, Captain R.L. Bond, R.E., has won the D.S.O.

The Bath munition workers' food protest on Saturday 19 January 1918.

On 26 January an article appeared in the newspaper concerning 'Aliens in Bath'. The story read:

Another Bath lodging-house keeper was fined at the Guildhall, on Friday, for failing to comply with the Aliens' Restriction Order by requiring her lodgers to register.

Minnie Toogood, of 11 Stanley Road, Manvers Street, was summoned for failing to require Frederick Crowther and Herbert Milton to register on January 1st as required by the Aliens' Restriction Order. She was further summoned for failing to keep a register during the past three months.

Defendant pleaded guilty.

Detective Inspector Marshfield said he called at defendant's house on Saturday and found that only two of the six lodgers had filled in their registration forms. She produced forms relating to two Russians and told him that she had had some Spanish lodgers but they had left. She did not know that an aliens' register was necessary.

The police record showed that six aliens had stayed at her house but registration forms had only been received for two of them.
   The defendant was fined £2 10s for each case.

In January, news was received of a Bath footballer who had been previously wounded in action. The report read:

Members of the Bath Football Club, and his fellow players especially, will be glad to learn that Gunner Edward Russell R.F.A. is recovering from the severe wounds which he received in September last. He was injured at Pilckem Ridge by shell, dropped by an enemy airman, and received seven wounds in the right foot, thigh, nose, shoulder, ankle, and the left foot, which was broken. Gunner Russell, whose home is in Paradise Street, Wells Road, enlisted early in the war. He is now at a military hospital at Manchester and able to walk with the aid of crutches. But it is feared that this fine forward will never play football again. Russell was one of the best men in the Bath pack and played for the county immediately proceeding the war. He is 25 years of age.

An exhibition of soldiers' work as published in the Bath Chronicle of Saturday 23 February 1918. The work was displayed at the Mineral Water Hospital and a visit was paid by HRH Princess Beatrice, who viewed the needlework of the soldiers who were all patients at the hospital.

Two soldiers proudly displaying their work during the exhibition at the Mineral Water Hospital during February 1918.

A recovering serviceman working on his needlework during the exhibition of soldiers' work at the Mineral Water Hospital during 1918.

On Tuesday 19 February, an exhibition of soldiers' work was displayed at the Mineral Water Hospital. A visit was paid by HRH Princess Beatrice, who viewed the needlework of the soldiers who were all patients at the hospital. Princess Beatrice, who was accompanied by her lady-in-waiting, Miss Bulteel, was welcomed to the hospital by Colonel Hendley P. Kirkwood, the chairman of the Board of Governors. The colonel accompanied Princess Beatrice through a double line of soldiers waiting in the hall to the exhibition room. Once there, the princess was presented with a bouquet, tied with heliotrope ribbon, by Sergeant C. Mackay Reid, RFA, who, as a member of the Household Cavalry, had been orderly for two years to the late King Edward. The matron (Miss Terry) and other ladies including Mrs Cave, who taught needlework to the soldiers, were presented to the princess, who then carefully examined the exhibits accompanied by Mrs Cave.

The *Bath Chronicle* reported:

The work was of a very meritorious character and included embroidery of conventional design, badges, cross-stitch work, chains of paper and beads, simple basket work and Teneriffe work. In addition to the many exhibits in competition, prizes being offered for the best work, there were many handsome complimentary exhibits. The badges were all excellent done but equally attractive was the fancy work, very noticeable being the representation of a garden and of a peacock, which took the prize in the King's landing section. There were various styles of note cases for sale and much interest was taken in specimens of the design, numbering seven, which are to form a super-frontal for the hospital chapel altar.

At the entrance to the hospital, Private Sloane was in evidence with his collecting tank which had been used to raise money. The tank had been constructed in the hospital, while Private Sloane had been a patient and he'd also built similar money boxes for two other hospitals in which he'd also been a patient.

The Victoria United football team photographed in February 1918.

The Guildhall. On Wednesday 20 February 1918, heads of many of the leading businesses in Bath assembled in the Guildhall to promote the scheme of building a destroyer. The mayor (Dr Preston King) presided over the meeting and proposed raising a sum equivalent to £2 10s per head of the population of Bath.

On Saturday 23 February, it was reported that Bath had been asked to raise £150,000 during the week of 4-9 March to pay for a destroyer. Lord Jellicoe, speaking in London on the previous Wednesday, said there was a shortage of destroyers and also a necessity to build more to cope with the German submarine raids.

The week of 4-9 March was styled as the 'Business Men's Week' of the National War Bond Campaign. On Wednesday 20 February, heads of many of the leading businesses in Bath assembled in the Guildhall to promote the scheme of building a destroyer. The mayor (Dr Preston King) presided over the meeting and proposed raising a sum equivalent to £2 10s per head of the population of Bath. The city had already subscribed £417,634 for War Bonds. General discussion took place at the meeting as events for the fundraising week were planned.

In February, a story appeared in the local newspaper under the headline 'Blind Soldier's Sight Restored'. The article read:

> *Seldom can the recorder of grim happenings of the war narrate a story so cheering as the story of Mr. George Fooks, of this city, who has regained his sight after three years of partial blindness. Mr Fooks, whose home is at Chard, but who now lives at 7 St. George's Place, Upper Bristol Road, was one of the earliest to volunteer for the front. He enlisted on September 5th 1914 and was drafted to the 1st/5th Somerset L.I. On April 26th, while practising trench digging at Prior Park, he was struck in the face by some earth thrown up by a comrade and blindness supervened. Before joining the Army, Mr*

George Fooks whose sight was miraculously restored. He lost his vision while practising trench-digging at Prior Park after being struck in the face by some earth thrown by a colleague.

> *Fooks was a carman at Chard, employed by the British Petroleum Company, and after his accident, he was trained at St. Dunstan's as a shoemaker and matmaker. Barely a fortnight ago, Mr Fooks was present at the opening of the Bath Photographic Society's Exhibition as a living testimony to the value of the training received at St. Dunstan's to which the proceeds of the exhibition were devoted.*
>
> *About a fortnight ago, Mr Fooks experienced pains in the head*

*and returned to St.Dunstan's where he was advised that this was a
sign of returning sight. This good news proved true, for on Tuesday
last week, he was trying to decipher a letter when he discovered that
his vision was returning and he has now the perfect enjoyment of
his sight. His delight is, of course, beyond bounds. The front of his
shop at St. George's Place records that he was trained at St.
Dunstan's – an inscription which will remind Bath for some time at
least of the good services of that hostel of healing and comfort.*

Fooks has this week voluntarily offered to rejoin the Army.

**Captain A. G. Henshaw dropping
literature concerning war bonds on Bath
during the beginning of March 1918.
Captain Henshaw was accompanied in
the air by Captain Nairs and Lieutenant
McKinnon.**

**Captain A. G. Henshaw of
the RFC. An
accomplished airman,
Captain Henshaw looped
the loop at a height of
only 500 feet over
Hedgmead Park, after
distributing leaflets over
Bath.**

At the beginning of March, three planes took part in an aerial display
dropping War Bonds literature and vouchers over the city. Witnesses
reported the most daring flying over Bath that has ever taken place.
Captain A. G. Henshaw was accompanied in the air by Captain Nairs
and Lieutenant McKinnon. The two latter officers operated their planes
at a height of 1,000 feet. On numerous occasions Captain Henshaw
descended amazingly low. At one point he passed across the Orange

Grove in level with the abbey clock and the third and fourth floor windows of the Empire Hotel. Afterwards, over Hedgmead Park, he looped-the-loop at a height of only 500 feet.

The miniature rifle range in the Drill Hall at Lower Bristol Road. The replica of the Ypres Front was constructed by Corporal Elwood and came complete with movable targets of model aeroplanes. The photo appeared in the Bath Chronicle of Saturday 16 March 1918.

The *Bath Chronicle* of Saturday 16 March carried the story of a miniature rifle range in the city. It read:

A very clever and most useful piece of work has been carried out by Corporal Elwood, at the 2nd Batt. SVR miniature rifle range in the

The Parade Gardens. The gardens featured many band concerts and other events throughout the war.

THE PARADE GARDENS, BATH.

G.44

Drill Hall, Lower Bristol Road. Corporal Elwood has constructed a replica of a section of the Ypres front, with a painted background, sand and sawdust fields, coloured to represent the different soils, and movable targets of model aeroplanes, guns and the impedimenta of war. The range makes the combination of visual training and actual firing practice a possibility and provides a means for the training of marksmen of the very highest utility. Corporal Elwood is constructing a smaller range at Midsomer Norton.

At the beginning of April, the *Bath Chronicle* reported the news that a prisoner-of-war had returned to Bath. The story read:

Second Lieut. H.E.B. Dickson, of the Devon Regiment, has been repatriated and is home in Bath after being a prisoner for a considerable while in Germany and subsequently in Switzerland. Lieut. Dickson was reported to have been killed in action on March 26th 1917, and mourned as dead by his relatives. Subsequently, it was learnt that he was wounded and interned in Prussia. He was injured in the shoulder, and the wound not being healed, he was recently passed by the medical board in Switzerland for repatriation much to his delight and that of his wife. Lieut. Dickson was married in Bath while on leave in 1916. He is an old Monktonian and was congratulated by many friends on his return to England at the school sports on Monday, when he demonstrated his vitality by winning the 100 yards Strangers Race in fine style.

On 6 April, the local newspaper reported of a Bath boxer's success. The story read:

News has just arrived of a glove fight in France between Sergeant Rogers, R.F.A., of 21 Maybrick Road, Oldfield Park, Bath, and Corporal Painter, D.C.L.I., in which Rogers scored a brilliant success, beating his opponent in the third round by a complete knock-out. Sergeant Rogers, who is a Bath lad, has once again shown his undoubted genius as a boxer. His record during the war and previously to it, shows a splendid average of wins. Sergeant Rogers is well known in Bath boxing circles and has figured in many contests being a familiar form among Stothert and Pitt's Athletic Club members and a frequent performer in their ring. He has been wounded and recently returned to the firing line, where the contest referred to took place.

The Pulteney Hotel. During May 1918, the Pulteney collected a total of £122 on one Thursday evening, which went towards the effort to raise £5,000 during the week to replace YMCA huts lost in the German offensive. It was stated that excellent contributions were being made by visitors to hotels within the city.

The *Bath Chronicle and Weekly Gazette* of Saturday 11 May reported on the effort to raise £5,000 during the week to replace YMCA huts lost in the German offensive. It was stated that excellent contributions were being made by visitors to hotels in the city with the Pulteney collecting a total of £122 on the previous Thursday evening. Proceeds from barrel organ collections in the street, hosted by children dressed as fairies, proved very satisfactory and house-to-house collections yielded many hundreds of pounds. Gifts for an auction had been donated as well as collections at local churches.

Miss Pow's pupils dancing at the carnival at Sydney Gardens during June 1918. The carnival lasted for three days and a total of £2,759 was collected.

An airman passing over Bath on the afternoon of Tuesday 14 May dropped a letter addressed to Mrs Milne of 66 Newbridge Road. The letter landed at the rear of 14 Johnstone Street, Laura Place, which was approximately a mile-and-a-half from its destination. The letter was discovered by Miss Trumper, who saw a piece of paper flapping against a back room window. As she opened the window to reach it, it flew off into the garden where she retrieved it. She found that attached to the piece of paper was a fairly large letter addressed to Mrs Milne and bearing 'O.H.M.S.' and 'Special Aerial Post', with a sketch of an Australian stamp that was hand-drawn. Miss Trumper immediately took the letter to the address to deliver it but found that Mrs Milne was out of the city. However, another Australian lady, who was her companion, took the message. It transpired that the communication was from a cousin of Mrs Milne. It was known that he was to be flying over Bath but it was not expected that he would try and communicate by letter. The *Chronicle* reported that this was the first time they had heard of someone dropping a letter from an aeroplane although distribution of trade leaflets and literature for War Bonds had been dropped previously.

On Saturday 25 May, the *Bath Chronicle* announced the forthcoming attraction of Broncho Bill's Wild West Exhibition. The story read:

As will be seen by an advertisement in another

An advert for Broncho Bill's Great Wild West Exhibition and Mammoth Circus which the Cricket Ground in Pulteney Road on Friday 31 May 1918.

column, Broncho Bill's Wild West Exhibition and Mammoth Circus is to pay a visit to Bath on Friday, May 31st. It will be located on the cricket ground and will be here for one day only. The exhibition is a representation in miniature of some of those features of life on the prairie which have gone to the making of so many of the breathless novels of our younger days. Some of the finest lasso throwers in the world will show their dexterity and clever whipstock crackers will appear, together with expert and experienced broncho busters. The Indian and cowboy's ride for life is well worth seeing but the greatest spectacle of all is the attack on the Deadwood coach, strikingly illustrative of the old days when fights between the 'Pale Face' and the Red man were of frequent occurrence. Among the special features are the great Royal Nik-ko Troupe of Japanese entertainers. The programme also includes male and female equestrians, troupes of daring acrobats, aerial gymnasts, beautiful performing horses and ponies, and funny clowns and mimics. The brass band will be in attendance. There will be two exhibitions daily, whatever the state of the weather. Every arrangement has been made for the convenience and comfort of visitors and the seating accommodation is for 5,000.

During June, a carnival was held in the Sydney Gardens that lasted for three days. The funds raised went towards hospitals and other local institutions. Altogether, a total of £2,759 was collected.

The Grand Pump Room. When American troops arrived in the city on 4 July 1918, they were met at the Grand Pump Room by the lord mayor and were entertained to luncheon in the concert hall. With the rationing restrictions, the meal had to be frugal but was enjoyed by everyone. The tables were decorated with flowers and each soldier was handed souvenirs of Bath.

On Thursday 27 June, the *Western Press* featured an article under the headline 'American troops to visit Bath.' The story read:

> *An invitation to United States troops to visit Bath on Independence Day has been accepted and a body of 300 American soldiers will be entertained in the city. The arrangements include a parade on the main streets, luncheon at the Pump Room, sports on the Recreation Ground and tea in the Institution Garden at the invitation of the Mayor.*

The American soldiers arrived at the railway station in Bath at 12 noon on 4 July. They were met by Alderman Cedric Chivers at a station a few miles outside the city and given a programme of events for the day. The Band of the 2nd Battalion Somerset Volunteer Regiment was waiting on the platform and, as the troops arrived, they played *The Star Spangled Banner*. With the mayor on the platform were the town clerk, two ex-mayors and members of the military forces and other dignitaries. Outside the platform was a florally decorated buffet and the troops were dispensed lemonade and other cooling non-alcoholic beverages. The band was accompanied by eighteen drums and bugles of the 1st North Somerset (Y.M.C.A.) Scouts under Scoutmaster Mayer. The brass band and bugles continued to play music throughout the soldiers' march through the city.

Major A. H. Fortt (commandant of the volunteers) and Captain J. S. Thatcher (Somerset Light Infantry) walked ahead of the band and the American troops, who were 196-strong. A huge crowd awaited them at the bottom of Manvers Street, outside the station. They cheered loudly while waving handkerchiefs, hats and small American flags. The raucous welcome continued as they marched onward through the streets. Their march began with *Marching through Georgia*, and this was followed by *Stars and Stripes*, *Manhattan Beach*, *El Capitan* and *Colonel Bogey*.

Over the abbey, the Guildhall and the Empire Hotel were displayed the Stars and Stripes while the two towers of the Grand Pump Room Hotel provided vantage points for the American flag and the Union Jack.

Children were intensely excited by the visit of the Americans and their arrival came in their school dinner hour so they were there *en masse*. Hundreds of them had flags and they not only cheered as the troops passed but followed them along on their march. On reaching Royal Victoria Park, the troops took a quick rest before marching towards the Pump Room, where they were welcomed by the mayor. The visitors were entertained to luncheon at the Concert Hall. With the rationing restrictions, the meal had to be frugal but was enjoyed by everyone. The tables were decorated with flowers, and each soldier was handed souvenirs of Bath.

The string quartette of the Pump Room Band played selected music and there were many toasts as well as a long speech from the mayor giving praise to our American allies. Luncheon was followed by a service at the abbey.

After the welcoming and planned events on 4 July for the American troops, a baseball match was played on the Recreation Ground. An article in the *Bath Chronicle* explained the rules of the game. The newspaper described the game as a mixture between cricket and rounders.

In the Institution Gardens, a garden party was held where the American troops, several hundred citizens and temporary residents were the guests of the mayor and mayoress. Tea was served on the terrace alongside the river. After tea, the company settled in chairs in shaded parts of the garden and listened to the music of the Municipal Orchestra led by Mr G. B. Robinson. Others strolled through the grounds. The musical programme included *Rule Britannia*, *Charlatan* and other popular music. Songs came from Miss Lily Morgan, who sang *Roses of Picardy*, amongst others. At seven o'clock, the orchestra played *Star Spangled Banner* followed by *God Save the King*.

After the garden party, the Americans visited places of interest in the city and at 8.30 pm assembled at the Roman Promenade and were served with sandwiches, coffee and lemonade. Cigarettes were also handed out. In the concert hall, the troops cheered the mayor and the people of Bath for their warm welcome. The soldiers fell-in outside the Pump Room and marched to the station, singing along the way, much to the delight of the crowds who had come to see them off. The *Bath Chronicle* reported:

When the men were drawn up, the Mayor spoke a few words, saying how sorry he was the time had arrived to say 'Au revoir.' He said everyone in the city had been delighted to see their American friends and his parting words were 'Good luck to you. God bless you all.' The troops acknowledged his Worship's remarks by rousing cheers. The Americans than marched to the G.W.R. followed by an immense concourse. The Mayor and Town Clerk went to the station and saw off the last of our city's memorable visitors, whose train left Bath at 9.15 pm amid a scene of great enthusiasm, there being large crowds on both platforms to wish them good-bye.

Crowds gathered in the streets of Bath to welcome the American troops on 4 July 1918.

A baseball match was played on the recreation ground on 4 July 1918 between the visiting American troops (shown) and RAF Canadians. The Americans won by 8 runs to 3.

The American troops pictured after luncheon at the Roman Baths on 4 July 1918. The troops received a tremendous welcome when they arrived in the city, with people lining the streets to see them.

In the *Bath Chronicle* of Saturday 6 July, there appeared an invitation to the women of Bath. The article read:

> *An appeal is made to the women of Bath, in an advertisement in this issue, to attend at the Guildhall next Monday at 5 o'clock, when a meeting will be held for the inauguration of the Woman's Recruitment Campaign in Bath for the Queen Mary's Auxiliary Corps and the Woman's Land Army. Mrs Ralph Durrand and a lady speaker from the War Office will explain the conditions of service in the former organisation and Mrs Hignett, of Southstoke, will speak on the need of women for land work.*

It was announced in the newspaper on 15 August that Mrs Winston Churchill was in the audience at the Roman Promenade on Thursday afternoon to hear Mr Augustine Birrell MP speak about the Red Cross collection of books for soldiers overseas.

The *Bath Chronicle* of Saturday 17 August stated:

> *Dr. J.J. Scales, of Bath War Hospital, has won a War Certificate for £1 in the draw arranged with Melksham Red Cross sale this week. The lucky winner of £100 5 per cent War Bond Stock was Mr. W.J. Diplock, of Ladydown Farm, Trowbridge, and the dairy cow offered as the second prize went to Mr. J. Ferris of Witcombe, Melksham.*

5618. The Circus, Bath.

The Circus. During August 1918, the amount of £34 0s 6d was raised in the Circus district of Bath on France's Day, which had been an annual event for the past few years. The money raised was sent to the French Red Cross.

The same paper, on the same day, announced that sales of National War Bonds had now reached £1,000,000,000. The chancellor of the exchequer pointed out that it was the largest subscription of money ever recorded for an issue, the last record being held by the British War Loan of 1917, which raised £948,450,000.

Later in August, the *Bath Chronicle* reported the consequences of a mustard-gas attack:

Much sympathy will be expressed with Mrs. Findlay, so well-known in Bath before her marriage as Miss Cecile Anderson, in the news that her husband, Lieutenant-Colonel J.M. Findlay, D.S.O., of the Scottish Rifles, figures again in the casualty list. He was gassed about a week ago and, unfortunately, the agent employed was of the worst form, familiarly known as 'mustard gas.' The patient is at present in hospital at Rouen but I am glad to hear that when his condition improves sufficiently, he hopes to be moved to England.

On Saturday 31 August, the *Bath Chronicle* carried the story of 'Aliens Interned from Bath.' It read:

A further official list of internments of enemy aliens based on the recommendations of Mr. Justice Sankey's Advisory Committee, was issued on Tuesday. Altogether about 300 orders for internment have been made but the police authorities have not yet been able to carry all of them into effect. Accommodation has to be found for these aliens and, at present, room cannot be provided for more than 15 per day. It is not convenient to send them to the Isle of Man and it is considered desirable that internment should take place in the neighbourhood of London where the accommodation is by no means limitless. Many of the aliens have been sent to Wakefield and others, both from the country and London, have been interned at the Alexandra Palace.

The following names appear in Tuesday's list:

Blass, Charles A.P., Bath. Aged 46. Twenty-four years resident with British-born wife. Was a head waiter.

Murscehel, Jacob Michael, Bath. Aged 48. British-born wife. A cabinet maker.

Watjen, Herbert George, Bath. Aged 42. Nine years resident in

England and seven years in Australia. He was formerly a licensed victualler and is now of independent means.

These three Germans were all interned, soon after the outbreak of war, on October 21st, 1914 but on December 2nd of the same year, they were set at liberty and allowed to carry on their normal lives. However, instructions reached the Bath police from London that these three aliens were to be re-interned and they were taken to Alexandra Palace on the 19th inst.

At the end of August, it was reported that a local man was discharged from the army due to wounds. The story read:

Sapper W. J. Hall, Wessex R.E., son of P.C. Hall of the City Force, has just been discharged from the Army as physically unfit. He was severely wounded at Salonika a year and ten months ago and has undergone five operations. The same shell that wounded him killed Sapper Porch, of Claremont Buildings. Previously, Sapper Hall was wounded in France, wither he went in 1914 with the Wessex. A younger son of P.C. Hall has been transferred to the R.A. in Palestine after being in General Allenby's force that captured Jerusalem, as a member of the R.A.M.C.

Mrs Robbins, who was on board the ill-fated Galway Castle. The Galway Castle was torpedoed at 7 am while on its way to South Africa. Mrs Robbins was one of the crew who was rescued and her story was later told in the Bath Chronicle of Saturday 21 September 1918.

Mrs Kaufman, who was rescued after the attack of the Galway Castle. Together with Mrs Robbins and Mrs Kennedy, the wife of Captain Myles Kennedy DSO, all three local women survived to tell the tale.

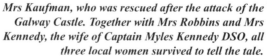

On Thursday 12 September, three women from Bath were on board the Galway Castle *when it was torpedoed at 7 am while on its way to South Africa. All three were rescued and were said to be no worse for their terrible experiences.*

One of the women rescued was a Mrs Robbins, who was the widow of Captain J. L. Robbins of the 10th Cheshires. It was reported that when the torpedo struck the engine room and broke the back of the ship, Mrs Robbins was in her nightdress, in her first-class cabin, and ran out to the corridor where she cut her feet badly on broken glass that had been smashed by the explosion.

The article was carried in the *Bath Chronicle* of Saturday 21 September and continued:

Mrs Robbins speaks of the behaviour of the many women passengers as simply wonderful. They lined up in their allotted positions without any approach to panic – luckily for them it was light – and as the boats were swung out, the women and children were placed in them. Some of the boats capsized and that in which Mrs Robbins found a place was turned over by the very rough seas. After a time, she was picked up by a lifeboat in which was the Hon. H. Burton, the South African Minister of Railways.

She remained in the lifeboat for about nine hours before being taken aboard a destroyer into which they were packed like sardines. Her thin night attire was supplemented by a jersey, some blankets, a pair of socks and men's boots (the latter not to be despised in the circumstances). The men, she declares, behaved perfectly splendid all through and did all they possibly could for the comfort of the women and children. On reaching Plymouth, the rescued passengers received a supply of clothes which had been sent down by the owner on the liner and, in some of these, Mrs Robbins made the return journey to Bath.

She told a Chronicle interviewer on Monday morning that she had lost everything she possessed in the world, as she was taking everything with her to South Africa. She literally had nothing but a nightdress.

In addition to her cut feet, Mrs Robbins sustained badly bruised legs and her arms also bear contusions, these, she explained, being caused by the men clutching her so tightly to keep her from being pitched out of the destroyer.

She speaks sadly of the distressing scenes that were witnessed, of husbands and wives and parents and children being separated, but derives considerable satisfaction from the fact that she was able to save two young children, a boy and a girl.

Two other local women who were saved were Mrs Kennedy, the wife of Captain Myles Kennedy DSO and Mrs Kaufman of 7 Argyle Terrace, Twerton.

Girls of the Somerset WAAC stationed at Christchurch near Bournemouth in October 1918.

On Saturday 19 October, Mr J. A. Bladwell, of Kingsley House, Upper Oldfield Park, received news from France of the death of his son, Leonard. The acting CO in a letter of sympathy wrote:

It was a dreadful and unexpected shock to us. He was killed by the fragment of a shell at about 8 am on the 14th inst. as he was waiting with his section to undertake some work in connection with recent operations. He had just seen to the safety of his men by placing them under cover and was discussing his plans with the sergeant when he was hit. He did not seem to suffer at all but quickly lost consciousness and died within half an hour. I had his body brought back to camp and with the whole of his section, and all of the officers of his company except

Second-Lieutenant Bladwell, who died on 14 October 1918. He was 26 when he died. He had been educated at Wycliffe College, Stonehouse. He joined the Public School Corps in October 1914 and was made a corporal in August 1915 before transferring to the RE Special Brigade and sent to France. In April 1918, he obtained his commission.

one, who had to be left behind on duty, we held the funeral in one of our military cemeteries. It was a sad and touching spectacle. Though he had not been with this company very long (about four weeks), we had all soon developed an affection for him and an admiration of his high principles, courage and sense of duty and we feel that we have lost a good comrade. His own section have made, and erected, a very nice little cross – the best they could – to his memory.

Second Lieutenant Bladwell was 26 when he died. He was educated at Wycliffe College, Stonehouse. On leaving, he joined the Public School Corps in October 1914 and was made a corporal in August 1915 before being transferred to the R.E. Special Brigade and sent to France. In April 1918 he obtained his commission.

Miss Violet Vanbrugh, who appeared at the Palace Theatre in a one-act playlet, The Woman on the Window Sill during October 1918.

On Wednesday 30 October, two American soldiers, who had died of wounds at the Bath War Hospital, were buried in Bath with full military honours. The first to be interred was Private Otis Douglas of the 119th USA Infantry who came from Stoney Point, North Carolina. He was 23 years old and was buried at Locksbrook Cemetery. From the Australians' No 1 Command Depot at Sutton Veny came a splendid band, which was in Bath to play at the funeral of a fellow Australian. They also played at the funeral of the Americans and, in front of the band, marched a firing party of the 2nd Volunteer Battalion Somerset Light Infantry under the command of RSM Sinclair. The same unit supplied the bearers. The band, upon reaching the Weston Hotel, commenced playing the Dead March and continued until they were in the cemetery. The coffin was draped in the Stars and Stripes and bore several wreaths. Volleys were fired over the grave and Corporal Bugler Wills sounded the *Last Post*. The second funeral was of Private William Foyle, who had died on 25 October aged 26.

When armistice was agreed between the Allies and the Germans, the fighting in Europe came to an end. It went into effect at 11 am on 11 November. When the news reached Britain, people throughout the land took to the streets to celebrate. In Bath, thousands turned out in the street to rejoice and the mayor was driven through the crowds of people on an open top bus.

An advert from Lipton's announcing that jam would soon be rationed. The advert appeared during November 1918.

The war had been a long and bloody one. Bath had played a major part in the struggle. With the war over, there wasn't a family in Bath who hadn't lost a son, father, nephew, uncle or brother. There were tremendous celebrations in the streets as the end of the war was announced but the effects of the conflict lasted for years to come. One old soldier from Bath, Harry Patch, would become the last surviving Tommy to have fought in the trenches during the Great War and would continue to tell his story until his death in July 2009 aged 111.

BATH'S NEW MAYOR & MAYORESS.

Councillor A. W. Wills.

Mrs. Wills.

Councillor A. W. Wills and Mrs Wills became the new mayor and mayoress of Bath at the beginning of November 1918.

The crowd at Buckingham Palace on Armistice Day. Thousands of cheering spectators waving handkerchiefs, flags and hats lined the streets to celebrate the end of the war.

Armistice celebrations with many happy faces and much flag waving. American flags were waved alongside British ones, and everyone was jubilant that the war was finally over.

A postcard celebrating peace issued after the Armistice of November 1918.

Select Bibliography

The *Bath Chronicle*
The Morning Post
The *Taunton Courier*
The Weekly Advertiser
The *Western Daily Press*

Index